THE WAY OF SERVICE

A Modern Framework for a Christian Morality

MARK P. AMBROSE

PublishAmerica
Baltimore

Hardcover 978-1-4512-7159-1
Softcover 978-1-4512-7160-7
PUBLISHED BY PUBLISHAMERICA, LLLP
www.publishamerica.com
Baltimore

Printed in the United States of America

DEDICATION

This book is dedicated to my best friend, Rev. Jerome Borski, OSB and to a very special person in my life, Sister Rose Vincent, SC.

I would also like to dedicate this work to dear friends Stephen Mascilo and Trevor Pinker, who have lived lives of exemplary service to others for the last twenty years and now, though they seem to have moved on to a life of leisure, will, I am sure, continue in service to all those with whom they come in contact.

ACKNOWLEDGEMENTS

During the course of writing any work, it is the contributions of many that enable one to be ensured that the work's content is clear and of value. For this I owe my most sincere thanks to William Davies and Scott MacDougall. Their critical readings for both content and grammar have ensured that what I wish to communicate is as clear and interesting as possible.

This book also owes its writing, in a very special way, to the Sisters of Charity of St. Elizabeth Convent Station, New Jersey. As a result of a previous project which I initiated with seven of the sisters now resident in the Villa, I came to understand the heart of these women's devotion to our Lord. This special charism is their willingness to be sent and to serve as they are commissioned and as the needs of the local church require. My work with the sisters resulted in a book centered on the lives of these seven sisters, *Writing Straight with Cooked Lines*, which I hope they choose to publish one day. The gift of their lives, as well as the many others of which these were but a sample, pointed me back to service as the heart of Christian life. It is thus in a special way that I wish to thank these sisters specifically and their larger community, for it is the dedication of these women that is, has been, and hopefully will continue to be at the very heart of our faith.

TABLE OF CONTENTS

Author's Note:
In the following work I have tried to be as sensitive as possible in the use of the masculine pronouns when referring to God. I have, however, found that in many cases this led to contortions of the text. I beg the reader's indulgence. I am not using this masculine case to assign a gender to God.

THE PRAYER OF SAINT FRANCIS OF ASSISI

Lord, make me an instrument of your peace.
Where there is hatred, let me sow love;
where there is injury, pardon;
where there is doubt, faith;
where there is despair, hope;
where there is darkness, light;
and where there is sadness, joy.

O Divine Master, grant that I may not so much seek
to be consoled as to console;
to be understood as to understand;
to be loved as to love.
For it is in giving that we receive;
it is in pardoning that we are pardoned;
and it is in dying that we are born to eternal life. Amen

FOREWORD

For a variety of reasons, the word "sermon" is not a particularly savory one to many contemporary people. It tends to conjure up memories of long, dry disquisitions on uninteresting topics, delivered in a tone that could often veer toward the moralistic, if not the outright condemnatory. Books and movies are filled with the image of the American preacher, breathing fire and brimstone, waving his (always his) arms about before a flinching and dispirited congregation. We hear the word "sermon" and begin having flashbacks to our high-school American literature courses, where we learned about Jonathan Edwards' "Sinners in the Hands of an Angry God" (and, sadly, not about the less frightening components of his vast oeuvre.) Anyway, no. We decidedly do *not* want sermons, thank you very much.

However, we seem to have forgotten, particularly here in the United States, that all of this is not traditionally what a sermon is. A sermon is simply a reflection on personal and communal conduct from a religious point of view. It does not need to be condemnatory. It does not need to be haranguing. In fact, sermons often succeed best when their words are uplifting and inspiring—or where words are not even employed. The Buddha, so it is said, once delivered a sermon that consisted of nothing more than holding up a flower before his disciples, which resulted in the immediate enlightenment of one of them, who responded with a subtle smile of understanding. The Buddha's simple teaching on how to live rightly and well, contained in that small and seemingly trivial act, had reached at least one of his hearers. And no threat of hellfire was to be heard—at least not that day.

Of course, generally speaking, words are pretty crucial in a sermon. In Christian settings, those words generally serve to open up the meaning of biblical texts for a congregation of people who have gathered to worship God, an act that very often includes time set aside for a preacher or a priest to reflect on what the Bible can or does mean in the context of their own lives.

If that is what a sermon can mean, then what we have in Mark Ambrose's latest book is a sermon in the best sense of the word.

In *The Way of Service*, the Bible, and particularly the Gospel—that is, the scriptures that pertain to the life, ministry, death, and resurrection of Jesus of Nazareth—are front and center. It is the Gospel that serves as the primary point of departure. As for a good preacher, the Gospel provides the texts upon which his sermon is based. The Gospel lies at the heart of his sermon on the human condition and the choices human beings make as they try to live good, decent, and faithful lives—in this specific case, as Christians, as followers of Jesus.

Like a good preacher, Ambrose approaches his task not in the way that many of us have come to expect, but quite the opposite. He refrains from engaging in monotonous, academic pontification, and from moralizing and condemning. Although, let it be said, he does this without shying away from an intellectual and learned point of view, or from taking a stand on the matters he feels require an impassioned treatment.

Like a good preacher, Ambrose ranges widely in exploring his subject. This is not a systematic, linear, academic treatise. It is a meditation, a rumination, on what the Bible tells us about God, about ourselves, and about how we are to make our way in the world. Doing this takes time and requires covering a good deal of ground. This is precisely what he does in this book.

Like a good preacher, Ambrose enlists philosophers, poets, political leaders, and popes to help take us through his ideas, each of these figures contributing perspectives that complement the insights of the biblical passages at the core of the work. Here, we find Albert Camus side-by-side with the Rev. Dr. Martin Luther King, Jr., and William Shakespeare at the same table as Evelyn Waugh.

Like a good preacher, Ambrose asks what the distinctively Christian way of being in the world is, and in developing his answer, touches on a tremendous range of topics. He travels from the complexities of human identity in religious and developmental perspectives, to the key existential questions people face (or choose to ignore); from the character and nature of the human person, to the idea of the self-as-becoming; from the need to reframe how we understand morality, to the social and political questions that are the context for all of our daily actions.

In essence, Ambrose tells us, we have a basic choice to make. We can opt to serve God, our fellow human beings, and the world, or we can choose to serve our own selves and interests. *The Way of Service* is his attempt to provide a moral framework for raising to consciousness the unspoken and often unnoticed ways in which we make that choice (or not). It is his call to each of us, from a Gospel-centered perspective, to choose to serve God, others, and the world, rather than our individual desires.

Again, like a good preacher, Ambrose calls upon us to self-reflection and self-evaluation in light of the Gospel. He asserts that we have largely fallen into the legalistic traps that ensnared the Scribes and Pharisees, judging the moral correctness of ourselves and others based on adherence to certain "codes of conduct" or supposedly biblical "laws," and that we need to look instead to Jesus, who advocated what Ambrose calls "rightness of disposition" or "orientation to serve"—an inner attitude or state—that judges morality in terms of the intentions of the heart as necessary to our right actions. He wants to shift his readers' perspective on the moral life away from one of "thou shalts" and "thou shalt nots" to a more holistic and interior understanding of the complexities and conundrums of moral life in a real world, one in which one size does not fit all. This does not mean he advocates a slide into relativism, however, nor an easy affirmation of current culture that would imply that "anything goes." On the contrary, in many ways, Ambrose's approach is deeply conservative (or at least highly traditional) and is sharply critical of contemporary society and mores.

In the end, like a good preacher, Ambrose provides in *The Way of Service* a great deal of food for thought. There are no easy answers, here, and it is unlikely that any one reader will either agree or disagree with every notion encountered in the book. This is as it should be! A good sermon does not pretend to have all the answers. The best of them simply ask in new ways the profound questions with which people of faith are called to wrestle, Jacob-like, throughout the course of their whole lives. The key, as this book reminds us, is to engage in that struggle with faith and in love.

Scott MacDougall is a doctoral candidate in theology at Fordham University. He holds a master's degree in theology from General Theological Seminary. He has worked extensively with various non-profit organizations and, most recently, to end the exploitation of vulnerable populations in the sex trade.

INTRODUCTION

Human beings have always formed myths that have aided men and women in understanding who they were and how they should live in community. Often, these myths also included gods or deities that not only gave a certain weight to societal rules, but also pointed to a source of justice that was beyond human control.

The Mesopotamians developed a complex theory of their gods based on the precariousness of their lives in the Tigris-Euphrates Valley. The Egyptians developed a theology that was both complex and impressive. Many now accept that it was the Egyptians, under the rule of the Pharaoh Amenhotep IV, who first came up with a monotheistic god. While this monotheism lasted through his reign of 17 years, it was quickly abandoned and the traditional polytheism returned after his death.

Judaism changed all this. Surrounded by polytheistic cultures, the Jews clung to a developing belief in the supremacy of their one God, The Lord. Through interaction with these surrounding cultures, such as the Canaanites, the Babylonians and the Egyptians, the descendants of Abraham developed a relationship with their God, based on the idea of covenant. The covenant idea was not unique. It probably resulted from their mingling with the surrounding cultures. But its development as a holy contract between God and the Jews (comprised of multiple tribes) emerged as unique, perhaps ironically because the covenant was repeatedly broken by Abraham's descendants and renewed by a faithful God. The very breaking and renewing of the Covenant contributed to Israel's understanding of God and their relationship with their deity. That is, Israel's disobedience—its acting against God's contractual law—was never dispositive of the relationship; it was the love of God for his people that was the bedrock of the covenant and that made it more than mere contract. Parallel to this "legal history" was the Jews' evolving understanding of this God. The wrathful God, who brings floods and plagues, emerged over time as an ever more merciful and loving father. This unique relationship, built on the infidelity of humanity and the ever-faithful and hopeful God, was given unique utterance in the reported discussion between Abraham and God over the fate of Sodom and Gomorrah.

Then the LORD said, "Because the outcry against Sodom and Gomor'rah is great and their sin is very grave, I will go down to see whether they have done altogether according to the outcry which has come to me; and if not, I will know." So the men turned from there, and went toward Sodom; but Abraham still stood before the LORD. Then Abraham drew near, and said, "Wilt thou indeed destroy the righteous with the wicked? Suppose there are fifty righteous within the city; wilt thou then destroy the place and not spare it for the fifty righteous who are in it? Far be it from thee to do such a thing, to slay the righteous with the wicked, so that the righteous fare as the wicked! Far be that from thee! Shall not the Judge of all the earth do right?" And the LORD said, "If I find at Sodom fifty righteous in the city, I will spare the whole place for their sake." Abraham answered, "Behold, I have taken upon myself to speak to the Lord, I who am but dust and ashes. Suppose five of the fifty righteous are lacking? Wilt thou destroy the whole city for lack of five?" And he said, "I will not destroy it if I find forty-five there." Again he spoke to him, and said, "Suppose forty are found there." He answered, "For the sake of forty I will not do it." Then he said, "Oh let not the Lord be angry, and I will speak. Suppose thirty are found there." He answered, "I will not do it, if I find thirty there." He said, "Behold, I have taken upon myself to speak to the Lord. Suppose twenty are found there." He answered, "For the sake of twenty I will not destroy it." Then he said, "Oh let not the Lord be angry, and I will speak again but this once. Suppose ten are found there." He answered, "For the sake of ten I will not destroy it." And the LORD went his way, when he had finished speaking to Abraham; and Abraham returned to his place. (Genesis 18:20-33)

This bargaining with the almighty seems to us not only strange but impudent. Even stranger, however, is God's willingness to accept the bartering based on fewer and fewer citizens of righteousness as a basis for saving this city which has been so steeped in sin. Thus, even this far back in the covenant relationship, God is willing to see past acts of disobedience based on God's hope and faith in but a few. Far later this "few" would become the one, God's Son who would bear our indiscretions for the forgiveness of all.

Increasingly, as a method of maintaining their unique identity, the Jews developed a complex legal code that they attributed to their God and to the covenants that were continually made and refined with Him. This notion of law was central to their capacity to maintain their unique identity, for the Jews faced constant, and sometimes brutal, threats to their very existence as a unique people. Hebrew scripture recounts frequent wars, exile, captivity and enslavement, during all of which adherence to the law gained significance as a way to guard against assimilation. As the law took on prevalence in every aspect of Jewish life, it was increasingly understood as having its source in God's will. The law embodied the expression of God's ongoing relationship with his people. Thus, the law, as God's explicit expression of the Covenant, became almost indistinguishable from who God was to the people of God. Within this context, a major reform of the Jewish concept of law, covenant and identity was to be introduced by an itinerant rabbi from Nazareth named Jesus bar-Joseph.

Our knowledge of this man Jesus of Nazareth comes from the Gospel traditions as well as the writings of Paul, the first apostle theologian, a former Jewish persecutor of this new reform. The gospels do not present Jesus as a rabbi who rejects the centrality of the law as essential to Jewish life. In fact, Jesus emphatically declares,

> Do not think that I have come to abolish the Law or the Prophets; I have not come to abolish them but to fulfill them. (Matthew 5:17)

This statement very succinctly identifies the heart of Jesus' objective. What makes this apparently clear statement somewhat tricky to interpret is the fact that the essence of Jesus' reform is in refocusing how the law was used by the Pharisees and Scribes of His day. Jesus focused on rediscovering the law's vital purpose in the relationship of God to the Jewish people, as opposed to the more literal obedience to the prescriptive aspects of the law. A telling example of this shift of focus is revealed in the often-cited conflict over the observance of the Sabbath as understood by the Jewish leaders of Jesus' day.

The Sabbath laws were quite clear. No work of any kind was to be done on this day of rest; instead there was to be a focus on God. In the Gospel of Saint Matthew the issue of the Sabbath law is presented very clearly,

At that time Jesus went through the grain fields on the Sabbath. His disciples were hungry and began to pick some heads of grain and eat them. When the Pharisees saw this, they said to Him, "Look, Your disciples are doing what is unlawful on the Sabbath."

He answered, "Haven't you read what David did when he and his companions were hungry? He entered the house of God, and he and his companions ate the consecrated bread—which was not lawful for them to do, but only for the priests. Or haven't you read in the Law that on the Sabbath the priests in the temple desecrate the day and yet are innocent? I tell you that one greater than the temple is here. If you had known what these words mean, 'I desire mercy, not sacrifice,' you would not have condemned the innocent. For the Son of Man is Lord of the Sabbath."Going on from that place, he went into their synagogue, and a man with a shriveled hand was there. Looking for a reason to accuse Jesus, they asked Him, "Is it lawful to heal on the Sabbath?"

He said to them, "If any of you has a sheep and it falls into a pit on the Sabbath, will you not take hold of it and lift it out? How much more valuable is a man than a sheep! Therefore it is lawful to do good on the Sabbath."

Then He said to the man, "Stretch out your hand." So he stretched it out and it was completely restored, just as the other. (Matthew 12: 1-14)

What we see played out here so clearly is Jesus' focus on the essence of the law which, in this specific case, was on keeping the Sabbath holy through not engaging in the ordinary labors of life. What makes Jesus' view of the Sabbath law so different from those of the other Jewish authorities is that Jesus never loses sight of the fact that the law, even this law, is grounded in the convergence of two critical dimensions of His view of the Jewish faith. The first dimension is in synchronization with Deuteronomy 6:5, which states, "You shall love the Lord your God with all your heart and with all your soul and with all your might." And the second dimension finds its source in Leviticus 19:18, "You shall not take vengeance, nor bear any grudge against the sons of your people, but you shall love your neighbor as yourself; I am the Lord." It is in the marriage of these two essential aspects of the law itself that the essence of Jesus' reform is based. It is an understanding of the human person as the core of God's ongoing love and concern and the law as a means by which humanity comes to understand itself, individually and in community. Jesus always approaches every person and every situation with the firm belief that the human person is an end in itself and that humanity is the very vessel of God's love and Spirit.

It is with this essential understanding of God as the loving Father and the human person as of supreme importance to the Father that Jesus interprets the law. These two dimensions of Jesus' understanding of the law and the covenant breathe new life into our understanding of God, the centrality of love of neighbor and the connection between that love and the worship of God.

As the early Christian community grew and over time developed into a more organized Church, it emerged into a much more legalistic Christianity. By the middle ages, the Christian Church in the west had broken from the Eastern Church. The Western Church, centered in Rome, developed a moral system focused on the human capacity to act from its free decisions. The moral system which thus emerged (especially from the Irish monastic tradition) was as legalistic in its approach as the Judaic traditions critiqued so directly by Jesus. This meant that morally significant actions were actually categorized by their perceived gravity. Soon, the common lay person was very familiar with the concepts of mortal and venial sin as well as active and passive sin, or what were commonly referred to as sins of omission and commission. In this way, a moral model was being formed that in many ways mirrored the law-centered model of which Jesus was so critical.

This book has as its objective to go back to the gospels and to develop a moral framework that puts aside the legalistic moral model and to develop a method for Christians to understand how to entertain the right actions and bad actions based on the method used by Jesus. This will require that we appreciate human actions within Jesus' concept of the authentic human being, open to the Spirit of God and imbued with proper self-love and love of neighbor. Anyone who has read the New Testament knows already that Jesus did not spend much time listing morally good and morally bad acts. What he did do was to present a method for discerning "the right way to live" and how we should see the questions of moral rightness and distortion.

What we are developing here, then, is a moral framework, a context within which to understand morality—questions of a right and wrong orientation—not as a set of opposed lists of dos and don'ts, but as a context from within which we may maintain a right relationship with a loving God, a God whom we know most intimately in the person of his son Jesus Christ and in his continuing incarnation in the people around us.

This framework is focused on service and is divided into two parts. The first I have called "non-*serviam*," taken from the Biblical account of Lucifer's fall from heaven and his declaration, "I will not serve." The second I have called, simply, "*serviam*" or "the way of service." Lucifer, of course, was declaring his refusal to serve God. But, as I have said above, our knowledge of God in this life comes, in great part, through his presence in the persons of other human beings. That God chose to become human, in the incarnation of Jesus, means that humanity has taken on a divinity in the same way that divinity took on humanity. Thus, the fundamental choice to serve or not to serve our fellow men and women is very much at the heart of our covenant with God. We propose that it is better to embody the law in this way than to follow it prescriptively. For Christians, this must be a critical element in the understanding of what it means to be "Christ-like."

Through this reflection and the development of a moral framework, we will be able to come to an appreciation of morality from a Christian perspective that will have both relevance to us in the twenty-first century and that will stay true to the development of an understanding of the human person laid out in *The Will to Love*, which preceded this book and upon which this reflection is built.

There is a marvelous hymn, whose words, drawing from the Prophet Micah and written by Albert Bayly, provide a fine jumping off point for our reflection on moral questions:

What does the Lord require for praise and offering?
What sacrifice desire, or tribute bid us bring?
Do justly; love mercy; walk humbly with your God.
Rulers of earth, give ear! Should you not justice show?
Will God your pleading hear, while crime and cruelty grow?
Do justly; love mercy; walk humbly with your God.
Still down the ages ring the prophet's stern commands.
To merchant, worker, king he brings God's high demands.
Do justly; love mercy; walk humbly with your God.
How shall my soul fulfill God's law so hard and high?
Let Christ endue our will with grace to fortify.
Then justly, with mercy, we'll humbly walk with God
(*The Hymnal, 1982,* Church Hymnal Corporation, NY, 1985)

CHAPTER 1

Charting Our Course

In the Christian tradition there has been little focus on "The Way" as the mechanism to living life to its fullest. While this concept of the "Way" is clearly expressed in the New Testament, it is also present in such esteemed eastern traditions as Buddhism where it is referred to as the Buddha Dharma. While it is a much broader scope than this book is taking, it is important to note that there exist many commonalities between these two traditions on a spiritual rather than on a religious level. The purpose of following "a way", which both spiritual traditions espouse, as essential aspects of any person desirous of finding themselves, their unique purpose, peace and actualization are essentially common across these divergent traditions.

In Christianity, Jesus explicitly refers to Himself as "the way, truth and life." (John 14:6) The objective of the "Way" is thus expressed in both traditions as the pattern of right living. Implied in these traditions is the existence of certain well worn paths which have been marked, described and shared by many of this world's saints, and prophets of God.

W. H. Auden's poem, which is also a well-known hymn, expresses the promise of following the way of service espoused in the Christian tradition most beautifully.

He is the Way.
Follow Him through the Land of Unlikeness;
You will see rare beasts, and have unique adventures.
He is the Truth.
Seek Him in the Kingdom of Anxiety;
You will come to a great city that has expected your return
 for years.
He is the Life.
Love Him in the World of the Flesh;
And at your marriage all its occasions shall dance for joy.
(W H Auden—1907-1973, *The Hymnal 1982*, Church
 Hymnal Corporation, NY, 1985)

As is apparent, the way is not lined with gold, filled with wonder and bliss itself. For the way, as right and true as it might be, will be a journey through our world, which we inhabit with all its dangers. What is essential is the promise made to all that if we have the faith and hope to stay true to this way we will arrive at our home of peace and joy.

Thus it is clear that the way is not always that of righteousness. Traditions are filled with descriptions of the well worn paths of self dissolution and death. Being cognizant of the differences between the Ways of fulfillment and the paths of dissipation as the two main divergent courses is essential. In fact it is this very objective that undergirds this moral framework.

Reflecting on the alternative "Ways" of life is a method of aiding each person in ensuring that they can both determine the nature of their unique journey while protecting themselves from the allures of false sirens. These sirens, whose illusory messages can pull one off the Way and lead one astray, ultimately to the loss of one's self, one's purpose and one's unique role in the unfolding of life. The paths of in-authenticity are not easy to spot nor are the initial experiences necessarily negative. For this reason we must keep a vigilant eye open and also be aware of the many snares or traps.

It would be naïve for anyone beginning this book to think that there is one right "Way" marked out and somehow impervious to the uniqueness of the individuals who make up the human community. The "Ways," while demonstrating uniform aspects, are at the same time not impervious to the uniqueness which each individual human person is. What makes losing our "way" something of which we are all capable, is the fact that the essential characteristics of our unique journeys are fabricated from our strengths and talents as well as our weaknesses.

The loss of our "Ways" seldom results from our choice to follow a path of abject evil, but from the slow subtle distortions in what may have begun as the right expressions of our following and developing our God given gifts and talents. The threats and temptations that are a part of life are thus very real and very effective because of the fact that they can appear at first as our moving in the direction of the good.

As with the paths of distortion and dissipation, the "Ways" of authenticity, inner peace and purposefulness also have definite signposts. These markers will also be uniquely matched to the uniqueness of each individual. In this sense there are multiple unique qualities of the "Way" which acknowledge the uniqueness of the individual set upon them. What is important is that we are clear about the essential aspects of the "Way" espoused by Jesus of Nazareth regardless of how these essentials are molded to respond to the uniqueness of the individual person.

For purposes of this reflection, the "Way" to the fullness of life will be divided into two main categories: the "Way" entitled "Non-*serviam*" or the "Way" of, "I will not serve." and "*serviam*". "Non-*serviam*" will be described with special attention to the role of the human ego. *Serviam* will be discussed via the unique human experience of the role of death in human existence. The two major delineations of *serviam* and non-*serviam*, while certainly a part of the rich tradition of our Christian faith, are artificial descriptors created to aid readers in grasping the essentials being presented for their reflection.

The concept of the ego will be essential in describing a significant contributor to which way we choose. The ego itself is not a moral concept, but its placement in one's world-view is. This placement—focus on self or focus on the other—is one of the markers of service. The ego is literally the translation of the Latin "ego," meaning "I." I do not mean to carry with it baggage from Freud or anyone else. It is merely used here to indicate the self-referencing "I." As such it will play an important part in delineating an aspect of the self that will be able to make clear certain pre-conditions within the self necessary for a moral being. The concept of ego being proposed for our use is inherently morally neutral regardless of what we are describing. This fact highlights that the ego, in and of itself, is an abstract concept which can effect one's orientation for or against the reality of service that is central to this moral framework.

Inherent in the teachings of Jesus is the fundamental truth that what determines who one is and the moral path one is on is essentially a discussion of interiority. Also inherent, however, is the way in which interiority is made known through actions in the world. It is for this reason that this reflection will use the concept of the ego in aiding us in grasping one's internal moral orientation. This means that, while the ego may be important in grasping moral dimensions of a unique person, it is not in itself the source or the cause of categories of good and bad, right and wrong. In fact, the ego is as critical in discerning "Non-serviam" as it is in the description of "serviam." Essentially the ego, as it is being used here, is the unique personal energy, vitality and orientation of the self each one of us is.

At this juncture a brief description of the role of key concepts which will be used as we proceed in articulating our moral framework is warranted. The first concept is that of the self. The self is the person that I expose to the world and other people through my actions. The self is also the way I think privately of who I am, who you are and of the world at large. These realities are not always in synchronization. When they are in synchronization we would describe a self as being authentic, when they are out of synchronization we would say that that individual is inauthentic. It is thus possible to be authentically evil. This means that the evil I demonstrate in my life is true to the distortion at my very center or a manifestation of a distortion at my center.

The ego, as we shall be using this concept, is meant to describe the individuated vitality that is at the center of my "self". The ego thus expresses my unique being as well as the orientation I have toward life, other people and thus inherently indicative of what I value. The ego is something that operates one way when one is an infant and should evolve as one matures. It is situated in space and time. The ego, in and of itself, is neither good nor bad or right nor wrong. It can, however, be subject to fundamental distortions, which can have a moral outcome for the individual.

Both the concept of the self and the concept of the ego will be essential in describing the "way" of non-*serviam*. The self is shaped and molded by the ego that it expresses. As a result it is essential that one understand the more subtle aspects of both this self and its underlying ego prior to proceeding to a detailed explication of the "Ways" themselves.

Finally, the focus will concentrate on the effect our choices can have on our families, society and ultimately our culture. The objective will be to demonstrate how maturation is key to the understanding of the self that each of us is and its ongoing development. Over time each of us will choose a "way" as the primary expression of who we are and who we ultimately want to be.

As is clear by now, non-*serviam* is the Latin phrase best translated as "I will not serve." It is the phrase attributed to the most magnificent angel created by God, within Judeo-Christian mythology; Lucifer (the light-bearer) and archangel is said to have uttered this posture of defiance of God as the ultimate act of pride and disobedience. As a result, Lucifer and those angels that desired to follow him were thrown from heaven. This mythology of Lucifer as the devil is developed in great detail in Milton's "Paradise Lost" which describes the prince of Angel's descent below the earth:

…Toward the coast of Earth beneath,
Down from the ecliptic, sped with hoped success,
Throws his steep flight in many an aery wheel;

Nor stayed, till on Niphates' top he lights.
(*Paradise Lost, Book III, 739-742*, Arcturus Pub. Ltd.,
London, 2008.)

Many years later, in James Joyce's *A Portrait of the Artist as a Young Man*, Father Arnall refers to Lucifer's horrific utterance of "non-*serviam*" to God as the clearest characterization of evil and the crux of all sin and pride. Father Arnall continues the description of this original rift in heaven by completing Lucifer's statement that it would be "Better to reign in hell than serve in heaven". The protagonist in the novel, Stephen Daedalus, who is desperately trying to find his way as an artist, a man of faith and as an Irishman, later echoes Lucifer in his own decision to follow the life of the artist, stating, "I will not serve that in which I no longer believe whether it call itself my home, my fatherland or my church." This ardent choice of the young Stephen has profound consequences on this young man and his life's journey. As once this articulation of Lucifer to God tore the fabric of the cosmos, so now in a similar way it was to tear Stephen's self into pieces which would require a lifetime of mending. (James Joyce, *A Portrait of the Artist as a Young Man,* chptr. 5, Penguin, NY, 1976)

In juxtaposition to this set of choices that continue to tempt all of us, is the choice to love, to give oneself to others as a choice based not on the self, but on the needs of the other, which we will refer to as facets of a life orientation of service. Leo Tolstoy was once quoted as having stated "The vocation of every man and woman is to serve other people." (http://forum.thefreedictionary.com/postst1437)

The great philosopher of the middle ages, Maimonides, whose thoughtful writings on all aspects of life also articulated his appreciation for the essence of "A Life of Service" when he stated:

> Anticipate charity by preventing poverty; assist the reduced fellow man, either by a considerable gift or a sum of money or by teaching him a trade or by putting him in the way of business so that he may earn an honest livelihood and not be forced to the dreadful alternative of holding out his hand for charity. This is the highest step and summit of charity's golden ladder.(http://thinkexist.com/quotation)

Many such famous and not-so-famous men and women have discovered in their lives the truth behind human existence which can be discovered or which may remain foreign and shut out through the free choice of our human wills. This truth concerning the purpose of life is discovered, in part, through the realization that human life is a journey. This journey is not merely the metaphor of the progression of time we all experience in living, but the deeper appreciation of the unique process of our ongoing creation in which each of us is the key player.

We have but touched on the periphery of this notion of "The Way" as descriptive of human existence and the role it can play in shaping the selves we are and the world in which we live. Service is not easy and the many alternatives to it are not dark and foreboding so as to make missteps easily identifiable. It is for this reason that discussing these fundamental choices is critical to aiding anyone concerned with making the most of their time on earth, not just for themselves, but for all those they touch as part of their unique journey.

Few of us wake up one day determined to live lives of in-authenticity, narrow heartedness and self preoccupation. Few of us would probably describe ourselves using these words. This does not mean that we have nothing to fear, as if the majority of us walk firmly along a path expressive of what we hold as most noble and reflective of who we wish to be. Good people can be misdirected. Good people can convince themselves of their uprightness and innocence all the while potentially beguiled and not on the "Way" which will bring them to being all that the Creator intended when crafting their potential. Unfortunately, misdirection in life and moral or ethical breakage does not require the external signs of a twisted frame and unpleasant dispositions. As it states clearly in the book of revelation, "So because you are lukewarm, and neither hot nor cold, will I spew you out of my mouth." (Rev. 3:16) It is seldom blatant evil, which one is faced with and which exposes its true repulsion and destruction; rather it is the spew of luke-warmth, which is descriptive of that which is most often deleterious to our beings, families and societies. This is true not just in itself, but due to the fact that often it is these lukewarm people who are most susceptible to the true evils that do make themselves known in our world.

Would that it were so convenient that what is evil and destructive would externally manifest its presence so that those with good will could clearly and obviously identify evil when it is before one. The belief that evil externally marks its bearers and makes its reality apparent was first promulgated as far back as the ancient Platonic Schools. It was a teaching which was the natural outcome of the fact that pure existence (Being), which is ultimate goodness beauty and truth, would thus deliver its flowers of perfection to all those who were so imbued. Sadly, evil men and women are externally indistinguishable from the most saintly among us. This truth makes the need for understanding the Ways and their characteristics even more essential to those desirous of staying true to *The Way of Service*.

As we progress in this meditation on *The Way of Service,* it is essential that we keep in mind the ever present freedom that is central to our natures and our wills, which give expression to this freedom. For the meanings we assign to situations, people, the world and our selves are the fountain of our actions and our words. Thus our actions, which should express our inner selves, are the outcome of these conscious or semi-conscious meanings we must come to own.

The last element of this introduction must address more than the previous reflection and its significant contributions to this book. It must also make explicit what is being done by articulating a moral framework and what is not being addressed accept as methods for elucidating the major points.

As we begin this opening section on the "way" of *non-serviam*, it is critical to keep in mind that we are not focusing on the moral significance of human acts *per se*, and yet understand human beings as essentially actors who express their existential reality in and through acts. Actions also can have the capacity to alter us, as when we consider sacraments, which are actions in which we can participate and which can efficaciously open us to the sacred, of which we may not even be totally cognizant. An approach such as this would not be a moral framework, but rather a morality. The first section, *non-*

serviam, is meant to describe an orientation that is possible for any human person during a part of their life or, in its worst case, a life in its entirety. While it will illustrate this orientation with specific examples, its purpose is only to make clear through those examples what a *non-serviam* orientation might yield.

Initially, an artificial construct centered on the ego and its place within an individual's existence will be put forth as a method for describing how this existential orientation could come about. In order to have this construct make sense, a certain focus on the development of the individual and the role of the ego and various points within that evolution will be used. This will enable us to be clear as to how an orientation of *non-serviam* could be developed and its many very real results both for individuals and the various societies that individuals create.

It is essential as we progress that the focus of this reflection on developing a moral framework be clear. Those who have studied theology or ethics might have a preconceived notion that this book will focus of morally significant issues, such as bio-ethics, moralities of war or an attempt to assess the death penalty against our Christian sense of the sacredness of human life. A moral framework is quite a different thing. A moral framework is the establishing of a context or milieu in which these more specific moral questions can be looked at with a certain degree of academic rigor. A framework is intent on bringing the background of these important moral explications to the fore and focusing on it. For Christians, this will mean teasing out the foundations of any Christian moral discussion by looking at the essential facets of Christian moral ways of seeing hearing and living. Specifically, it is a reflection that will expose the moral backdrop of Jesus' and the early church's understanding of the dimensions of any moral discussion.

PART 1

Non-serviam

CHAPTER 2

Non-serviam:
The Subtleties of the Ego & Self

As was previously noted the concepts of the ego and the self are key in aiding in the description of how we end up on one path or another. Think of the ego as the unique, indivuated underlying vitality which gives expression to each individual. In this way a self which is narcissistic, spoiled, and manipulative in pursuing whatever is desired might be said to be ego-centric. This common expression exposes an underlying life orientation pre-occupied by one's own needs and wants.

One might describe another individual with characteristics almost opposite to the character described above. This person is focused on others and is attuned to the needs of everyone with whom they come in contact. This person lives a life of personal generosity, and self giving. We would describe this person as someone who is "selfless". Unfortunately, this common phrase is not as helpful in driving home the proposed role of the ego.

In the above simplistic descriptions, the ego is being described as the underlying vital energy of each human life. Two main results of how the ego operates have been described. The ego, while being the same life force in both individuals, gives expression of a self-centered person in one case and a selfless person in the other. What is the cause of the differences?

In order to make this clear it will be necessary to use a spatial metaphor containing the self. In the initial description of the self-centered person, the individual ego occupies the center of the self. For this reason the ego is oriented singularly to the self and its needs. In the second scenario the self-less person also has an ego as their life force, but in the case of this individual the ego is not at the center of who they are.

When the ego is not operating from the center of one's being, the question that arises first is: What is central? Some individuals choose to live with God at the center of their lives. As a result, they live their lives such that the values of God's teachings shape who they are, their openness to reality, and how they act. In fact, one might say of this type of person that they live in such a way as to see the world and the people they come in contact with as God would see them.

There is yet another option. Some people live their lives placing a particular ideal or political view at the core of their self. An example might be the humanist who places a notion of the supremacy of the human person at the core of their self and seeks to live a life that is true to this particular orientation. Humanism can and often is mistaken for a faith based orientation, but this is not necessarily the case. Humanism does not have to be, nor is it often, a path based on faith. Humanists can be wonderful people. They can also be influenced by particular political movements which can influence a way of being very far from a faith based life.

The construct of the ego as the unique expression of one's individual life and the use of the metaphor of space to speak about how our egos can contribute to the kind of person we may be, enables us to begin our reflection on the moral dimensions of the human person. This construct is merely an artificial way of thinking about ourselves which will aid us in formulating a moral framework as well as aid us in being able to assess potential moral dimensions of life and our choice to live from our ego orientation or not.

It is essential that, as persons most concerned with ensuring that we are on the right path and that we can recognize certain symptoms of distortion within ourselves, that we remember it is always the internal disposition, that finds its ultimate expression in our words and actions, which manifests who we most truly are. The following parable from Jesus is an example of the discontinuity that can exist between one's internal dispositions and the appearances of external actions when they are out of synchronization.

He also told this parable to some who trusted in themselves that they were righteous, and treated others with contempt:"Two men went up into the temple to pray, one a Pharisee and the other a tax collector. The Pharisee, standing by himself, prayed thus: 'God, I thank you that I am not like other men, extortioners, unjust, adulterers, or even like this tax collector. I fast twice a week; I give tithes of all that I get. 'But the tax collector, standing far off, would not even lift up his eyes to heaven, but beat his breast, saying, 'God, be merciful to me, a sinner!'I tell you, this man went down to his house justified, rather than the other. For everyone who exalts himself will be humbled, but the one who humbles himself will be exalted." (Luke 18: 9-14)

In this pericope, Jesus is articulating the reality, which we are trying to explicate, that what is essential is the source within us as critical in understanding the action without, not the mere observance of the action itself. Throughout this entire reflection the linkage of our inner dispositions as key to actions will continue to be of utmost significance as the only method of avoiding the curse of legalism railed against by Jesus.

In another place, Jesus makes this point even clearer by referring to the Pharisees and Scribes of his day as "whitewashed sepulchers" full of dead men's bones on the inside, but whitewashed on the outside. In this way, Jesus described their inner lives as dead, while their external lives, the lives exposed to the world for the view of others, seems exemplary.

Human beings are clever. They can fool many into believing what they want them to believe. It is thus critical for us to distinguish between who we are to others and who we are to ourselves and to God. It is for this reason that we are spending time on ensuring that there is a proper appreciation for the many aspects of our humanity. For without this process we may not appreciate our freedom along with the wonder and mystery of our beings and thus the same sense of wonder and awe for the lives of those around us.

At the core of this reflection on of the human person is acceptance and respect for each human being as a moral agent. Our moral agency is the outcome of our capacity to will and to do so freely. Another critical element of our moral natures is the reality that each human person seeks the good, both for itself and the other, the same way that each flower attempts to stay in direct alignment with the sun. Unfortunately, this natural good disposition is vulnerable especially in its periods of development. It is for this reason that understanding both human proclivities and as how these natural proclivities can be misguided is so important.

Another critical element of being human is the fact that each individual is a process of becoming. This process is not linear as is our aging, but recursive. At its core, the process of becoming as essential to our natures is a mystery as well as something to which each of us is called to be active participants. It is in this way that we must come to accept ourselves and each other as an ongoing response to life and to God, which becomes the essence of our personal narratives. This truth is absolutely essential to how we appreciate ourselves and others. It is a particular view of the human person which is at the heart of our inability to categorize ourselves and our neighbors. This fundamental respect for our ongoing unfolding is the basis of our ongoing capacity for metanoia or conversion. At the same time this ever real possibility of conversion makes judgment of ourselves or others unacceptable.

Many modern Christian theologians such as Stanley Hauerwas have stressed the identity of the person as a narrative which enables westerners to grasp the idea of the self as a non-static thing, but as a process of both becoming aware of and expressing the unique narrative that one is. It is the development of this unique story that expresses not merely the events of one's life, but more essentially the meanings that stitch these experiences together and articulate how one is becoming and what core realities are essential to that process. Character development in a narrative is an ever changing and evolving response to life and the ways of perceiving, which reflect the meanings most indicative of the persons we are becoming. It is from these meanings that our actions and our words evolve.

Our individual human identities are thus immaterial and in constant flux. In this way personal identity must be appreciated as the outcome of the uniquely human capacities to will and to do so freely. Our identities are thus tied to our experiences, our imaginations, thoughts, dreams, disappointments and sorrows as well as the central capacity within each of us to tie all these fragments together via the meanings we choose. In this way each human being is a process, or the evolution of one's unique and unrepeatable story. It is this concept of human identity as the creation of our individual narratives that is at the heart of our nature as moral beings.

Specifically, this means that the self, as it will be used going forward, is not a thing, but a verbal reference to a specific individual who is an ever changing process of becoming. The concept of the ego is thus not an attempt to deny this dynamic nature of our humanity. The ego will be used to describe the unique life force as well as the specific orientation which this personal life force can take. As such, the ego as it is being used here is a morally neutral concept. This appreciation of both the self and the ego should be understood as a reference to the unique identity of an individual which expresses the unique life force within them which is an important aspect of the creation of one's unique narrative.

This is not to suggest a kind of existential pointillism where each moment is radically distinct from the previous. Rather, the image I would like to suggest would be more one of a flow where our lives progress from one moment to another introducing the possibility of surprise and novelty and yet containing traces of the past we are to mix with this. This past may indeed be re-appropriated by new meanings or may linger as residual waste. We are ultimately the narrative which expresses to ourselves and to the world both that we are and who we are. This self is thus always coming into being and fading away. This concept of the self is the result of a deep appreciation of the individual as an ever changing, ever dynamic process, which expresses the unique life force at one's very core. Our individual life story is also our ongoing facility to be open to the call of our creator in and through life's events. It is these life events that are the possibility of conversion or actual conversion to which each of us is called throughout one's life. For this reason the perception of the self as a stagnant entity is a distortion. That distortion is essential in describing the misnomers associated with modern western concepts of the human person.

This initial conception the self is first and foremost the illusion of unity which is the result of our lack of appreciation of the rich nature we have been given. Our naïve experiences of our bodies and our memories and the cultural intellectual inheritance from the Enlightenment have encouraged the very forceful proposition that each of us is at our core a static reality which thinks, laughs cries and hopes. This error in the very manner in which we perceive ourselves denies our ever renewable selves not stuck determined by the past, but always capable of re-creating ourselves. The next moment or day always offers us the hope and capacity to begin drawing ourselves anew with the Grace of God.

The concretized illusion of the self is not required to explain the unique individual each of us is. It is in fact a distortion, for it solidifies that which is by its nature fluid. It postulates a thing as the required explanatory element of our subjectivity demonstrated in a life of endless change. This postulation of a static thing is not required. The self can be fully appreciated as a process of unfolding or becoming.

As the philosopher Ockham taught, the simplest explanation is always the best. Ockham saw many examples of convoluted explanations for particular realities that were maintained as a method of holding onto a certain way of thinking. An example where Ockham's theory of simplicity of explanation being the best would ultimately prove true would be in the debate between the geo-centric universe and the helio-centric universe. Mathematicians of Ockham's age spent years developing convoluted equations which attempted to explain the motion of the heavenly spheres based on the earth as the center of the universe. Once this postulation was later let go and the sun was placed at the center, these equations were significantly simplified. Galileo was then to prove, through the use of his lenses, that what the mathematicians were able to show via equations could be demonstrated empirically demonstratable via observation. This and many other examples led Ockham to grasp very clearly that if a simpler explanation could be provided and still explain the reality being focused upon then by its very nature it demonstrated its superiority to the more complex hypothesis.

There is no need for this static self as an identifiable thing to explain our experiences and the richness of the unique lives each of us creates. Our real identities are the expressions of our unique life forces and the ongoing exercise of our freedom through our capacities to will or establish a set of meanings which become the various threads that run through the narrative of our lives.

The self, I am, is experienced in the ever renewable now. When an infant is brought into this world its sense of itself is nothing more than that which is hungry, cold or terrified. The self, which is a much later abstraction, begins its process of discovery through its initial experiences of others, which will be the basis for the development of a much richer sense of self as the complementary side of the dialogue as the other matures. As a result, the early self (as in early childhood) desires to acquire its needs and in time to control the other as that which satisfies its needs. It is through this interaction of our primitive selves and the other that our individual identity slowly emerges. It is through this initial infantile process filled with fear and needs that the world of objects is discovered and simultaneously, the subjectivity of the infant evolves.

Initially, the infant is an ego-centric being that is served by often indistinct others. Only in time does this infant discover that it has an increasing capacity to serve itself. At the same time those indistinct others take on more distinctness and the young child can now recognize and prioritize others with respect to itself. The initial dynamic of coming to appreciate who I am in infancy and who the other is as "mother" (or her substitute) is the unfolding evolution from my appreciation of myself as a vague source of needs into my identity as an acting subject. The ongoing discovery of the other (first the mother) as first an object and then as a subject is a progression of the infantile mode. Initially, the infant will take time in accepting others as subjects and will manifest behavior that may be seen as cruel in its lack of appreciation for the unique needs of the other.

Through ongoing socialization the child will be trained to understand its own capacities as well as its own power. Only through training will the child also learn self control. In this process of discovery of self and others the child will come to face its own ego-centrality and the need to curb its lack of consideration of others through the corrections it will be subject to from others and its enlarged awareness. Teaching the child to share and to not bite or hit another child are all aspects of molding the child. In time, the child will also become more sensitized to its effects on others and thus come to realize a deeper sense of its capacity to act and its acts as consequential. Part of early childhood is the reality of the ego as central to the child's experience. An objective of childhood training is to encourage the child to let go of their ego-centricity, which was accepted as normal in infancy, but became increasingly less appropriate as the child matures.

Implied by this position is the fundamental belief that the ego, which does not have to be at the center of the self, ought not to reside there. In releasing its central place to something other, the ego is recognizing its essential distortion as the source of our perceptions, actions and our belief that our infantile manners of behaving are the best methods of getting our needs met. Purely for clarity, the child's desire to be the center of attention is part and parcel of the natural desire to control its world, which is both illusory and inherently distortive. By so doing, the child attempts to assert its primacy in opposition to the reality that we are members of a community of other subjects with equal rights to having their needs met.

The place of the ego is essential to the kind of individual one is and is likely to become. It is thus important to note that the ego's placement and not the ego is that which is a morally significant descriptive concept. It is the ego at the center of the self which is being declared as being out of place. This fact suggests that one should be able to understand what, if anything should be at one's core. Immaturity is often a label for individuals who have not come to replace the ego at the core of their being and thus those who act in manners that appear to be below the expectations of their age and experience. While normal development should enable children to emerge from selfish ego-centric lives, it is not the case that this transformation is inevitable. In order for this maturation to occur, the child must experience the world as safe.

The centralized ego has as its primary focus the self one is and one's personal needs. The distorted ego described as ensconced at the center of who I am has a single and unwavering point of attention, sympathy, concern and perception composed of the various needs, wants and desires of the self it expresses. Its characteristics are thus best described as a grasping and clutching orientation to the world. The ego-centric self can only perceive reality from the perspective of its own wants and needs. It focuses the energy of the ego on controlling reality and on fulfilling its individual desires. If such an individual appears to be centered on another it will most often only be as an extension of its own individual needs.

An example of ego centricity is the person whose attentiveness to life is most focused and attuned to reality as a method of self preservation, self promotion, and the creation of the correct perception of the self by others. It is an orientation of control and manipulation. In such cases the person is truly blind to those people, situations and things that are not central to the self's ego-satisfaction or protection. In some cases the individual may respond to a situation or individual in desperate need, but this is most certainly based on the ego's need for self satisfaction or, in some cases, for the creation of regard by others. It is thus not always easy to ascertain such distortions either in oneself or others, as it requires a maturity of self that would facilitate such self assessment.

A simpler and more general way of expressing this is that my ego-centric self is focused on my satisfaction alone no matter how altruistic any of my actions may appear. This satisfaction is relevant to all aspects of my being. This fact was recognized in the New Testament by Jesus when he contemplates those of his time who liked to be noticed in their acts of prayer, fasting and alms giving.

> Jesus said to them, "Watch and beware of the leaven of the Pharisees and Sadducees." And they began discussing it among themselves, saying, "We brought no bread." But Jesus, aware of this, said, "O you of little faith, why are you discussing among yourselves the fact that you have no bread? Do you not yet perceive? Do you not remember the five loaves for the five thousand, and how many baskets you gathered? Or the seven loaves for the four thousand, and how many baskets you gathered? How is it that you fail to understand that I did not speak about bread? Beware of

the leaven of the Pharisees and Sadducees." Then they understood that he did not tell them to beware of the leaven of bread, but of the teaching of the Pharisees and Sadducees. (Matthew 16:6)

Jesus is clearly warning against the doing of "good things" to be seen and noticed by others only, for in truth as a foundation for doing good, these action express the heart of the distorted self. The ego-centric self also parses out its generosity, care and concern to those it deems critical to its own well being and furtherance. As such, these public acts for public observation can be merely expressive of the ego seeking its own satisfaction.

When this separation between the internal dispositions and the external actions exists it displays the lie that has taken root deep within the human person. The flagrant manipulation of people and situations for the sole purpose of ensuring the promotion of the ego-centric individual is a danger that has shown itself to be almost limitless in recent history. The moral concerns for this all too human distortion is not merely limited to the source disease of ego-centrism, but also to the lies that must be spun around it as a method of concealing the truth.

The disposition of the self whose ego operates from the center of its being is thus at its base an orientation of self preoccupation. As such, it is manifest in how I am with myself as well as with others. For this reason what one attends to, what one aspires to and what is important will all be ranked based on the self achieving its particular desired ends. If the individual about whom we speak does not have need for something or someone, it is likely that neither this particular thing nor person will grab their attention. What is significant about this stance is that the ego centered self perceives the world as comprised of one type of reality, objects and in particular objects for the self's ongoing satisfaction and protection.

Another common distortion of the ego centered self is the inordinate desire to control all aspects of reality as the primary mechanism for achieving the goods deemed important. Through manipulation this truly pernicious life orientation can be concealed and can even be made to look as if it were the opposite of what it is. While the symptoms of this distortion are not unknown to most of us, such things as the gravitation toward those with power, the focus on its acquisition for oneself as well as the symbols of power are also not uncommon. Power plays a most significant role in this distortion because it provides what appears to be the greatest possibility of controlling reality. The New Testament identifies this tendency in the pericope concerning the foolish rich man,

And He spoke a parable to them, saying, The ground of a certain rich man brought forth plentifully. And he thought within himself, saying, What shall I do, because I have no room in which to store my fruits? And he said, I will do this. I will pull down my barns and build bigger ones, and I will store all my fruits and my goods there. And I will say to my soul, Soul, you have many goods laid up for many years. Take your ease, eat drink and be merry.

But God said to him, Fool! This night your soul shall be required of you, then whose shall be those things which you have prepared?

So is he who lays up treasure for himself and is not rich toward God.(Luke 12:16-21)

In this short pericope Jesus sets up the distorted life of a man clearly manifesting an ego distortion. In this instance a rich farmer's land has brought forth even more bounty for him. While he is already noted as being rich, this additional bounty does not evoke in him the desire to share some of his abundance with those in need, but gives rise to his plan to pull down his barns and storage silos so that his even greater abundance can be accommodated. A typical symptom of ego-centricity, which is the inability to be attuned to anything outside of one's individual interests, is confirmed.

In this story we have the absurdity of a rich man ripping down his barns and silos so that he can hoard even more, thus expanding his abundance even further beyond his real need. The question thus arises, why would he make the decisions he is making? It is certainly not based on need. What this story does not focus on, but what is certainly behind the actions of this wealthy farmer, is a demonstration of the close linkage between wealth and power. More yield from his orchards and fields is not required because he is already wealthy. The taking down of his store-houses and the building of even larger symbols of his wealth will surely make clear his increased surplus to all those around and thus make clear the perception of his increased power.

In having the wealthy farmer demonstrate his distorted life through the decisions he made as well as his self congratulations which entailed his sitting back and taking his ease, the conclusion of this story shocks us all the more. For in the face of this great wealth, increased power and self satisfaction, the imminence of this wealthy man's death makes clear his existential vulnerability regardless of his wealth and power.

The wealthy farmer also reveals the well worn truth that in having, with a grasping orientation, I both am attached to my bounty and obsessed with its potential loss. In this way I am a prisoner of that which delights me and brings me an artificial sense of security. Like the foolish rich man the effort to protect oneself from the reality of the mystery of my ever evolving self through valiant efforts to control and to hoard will not and cannot protect me from the flow of life.

So the issue of where one can find peace or contentment is raised for our consideration. Certainly, peace and inner contentment will not be found through the amassing of wealth. For Jesus the only answer is in facing the source of one's security.

> So do not worry, saying, 'What shall we eat?' or 'What shall we drink?' or 'What shall we wear?' For the pagans run after all these things, and your heavenly Father knows that you need them. But seek first his kingdom and his righteousness, and all these things will be given to you as well. (Matthew 6:31-33)

And in another place:

> Anyone who loves his father or mother more than me is not worthy of me; anyone who loves his son or daughter more than me is not worthy of me; and anyone who does not take his cross and follow me is not worthy of me. Whoever finds his life will lose it, and whoever loses his life for my sake will find it. (Matthew 10:37-39)

Both of these short teachings have as their central theme the need for us to let go, to accept our place as journeyers who neither can control nor escape life's unfolding. Jesus grasped so very keenly our tendency to want to cling to things, people, successes and the perceptions of others. As a result we are at war with life. We are self absorbed. Jesus repeatedly begs His disciples to embrace a new orientation in their relations to people whom they love and who love them. He is not asking them not to love them, but to discover the truth that is before them and to embrace it in its primacy. It is an appreciation that real love does not cling to the beloved, nor does it seek to absorb the beloved as a method of escaping the aloneness associated with our individuality. He even asks them to let go of their lives, as their own, or potentially another's. He also makes clear that only by giving one's life up will one find it. Often this finding of one's life has been interpreted to refer to its discovery in the hereafter. Consider rather, that it may be meant for discovery of one's true self in this world and as part of this life's experience.

This first delineated aspect of the individual who has chosen ego distortion is that they exist in a world of objects. When any individual experiences the world as comprised of objects, they also view that same world as at their service. Objects can rightfully be used, manipulated and made slavishly to serve the ego-self as either direct or indirect objects of the individual's desire. Objects are there to satisfy the subject, as food, as mechanisms for self promotion or to meet any and all of the needs and wants of the ego-centric self. The ego-centric self expresses its way of being in the world as one characterized by the actions of grasping, using and disposing of, and in an infantile way sees the world (composed of people situations and things) as merely an extension of itself to which it feels a strong sense of entitlement.

Another indicator of ego distortion is manifest clearly in the human proclivity to objectify and judge each other. If we truly appreciated ourselves as ever fluid and always open to the possible redemptive transformation which will be discussed in more detail later, then both our need to judge ourselves or the other harshly would be far less fervently expressed. Again this truth is articulated clearly in the New Testament with Jesus' command,

> Do not judge, and you will not be judged; and do not condemn, and you will not be condemned; pardon, and you will be pardoned (Luke 6:37)

Here Jesus is saying so much more than many realize. Jesus is accepting the inherent reality of each human as a process and thus not static. It is for this reason that no action can ever express the fullness of one's being for better or worse. Judgment and condemnation are acts of a rigid static ego articulating its distorted attempt to control and box in the other—as it has itself. It is certainly directly in opposition to the Christian spirituality that sees the ongoing unfolding of the individual as the most sacred process of life, and the ongoing response offered to each of us to see the sacred in the unfolding and choices with which we are ever being presented.

The ego distorted individual does not have to be a person lacking in social graces or unlikable. In many cases ego distorted people are very social and very much liked by those with whom they are acquainted. It would be a mistake to assume that the ego distorted person is anything less than very astute as to how the objects in his or her world (including other people) are critical in his or her achieving whatever they feel is needed, wanted or desired. A good analogy of the ego distorted person is the game of chess. In chess, while each piece on the board can be critical to achieving the positive outcome of the game, the actual worth of any piece is really determined by the situation on the board and often the pieces, regardless of their potential power, are sacrificed for the greater good of the ultimate checkmate. In reality the only piece on a chess board that has the same criticality at all points in the game are the kings, who provide a solid metaphor for the ego distorted self.

This appreciation of the ego distorted person is one who sees situations and people as dispensable elements in one's single-minded goal, which is to achieve whatever end is deemed most important at any moment. Ego-centric people thus are often very effective at playing politics and staging situations which they believe will reward them with the desired outcome. In this sense one can understand the Christian notion of the self as both ephemeral and yet real.

St. Paul opined on the distortions of the self that can infest one's life and the life of society in a letter to Timothy. Many of the repercussions of a distorted self were specifically outlined in St. Paul's list of the characteristics of the last days. Not only are the predictions frightening, they are also descriptive of many facets of our culture today.

But understand this, that in the last days difficult times will come. For people will be lovers of themselves, lovers of money, boastful, arrogant, blasphemers, disobedient to parents, ungrateful, unholy, unloving, irreconcilable, slanderers, without self-control, savage, opposed to what is good, treacherous, reckless, conceited, loving pleasure rather than loving God. (2 Timothy 3:1-5)

In this letter, St. Paul depicts a future in which the ego distortion is clearly manifest. It is a time of concern for him and the church as it proclaims a serious internal disfigurement that can pull one away from the life espoused by Christ and essential for personal and public peace.

It is most interesting that the first step in the eight-fold path of Buddhism is "right vision". This has a definite correspondence to our acknowledgement that only the non-ego-centered self can truly perceive reality as it is in its truth. Right vision entails the profound reality that being open and receptive to the world and the self are acts of generosity if they stem not from my wants needs and desires, but from my generous orientation to engage and to be attentive. But as the Buddhist concept grasps it, there must be an attentiveness, which seeks to experience reality as it is outside of ego-centric needs, wants and concerns. Christianity agrees with this and expresses this truth in numerous quotes from Jesus in the New Testament. In the following pericope, Jesus focuses on the right seeing that is both humble and non-ego oriented.

Why do you see the speck that is in your brother's eye, but do not notice the log that is in your own eye? Or how can you say to your brother, 'Let me take the speck out of your eye,' when there is the log in your own eye? (Matthew 7: 3-4)

The orientation of judgment described so clearly above is a distortion wherein one's attentions are focused on the imperfections of everyone else. By focusing on the imperfections of others the authentic self attempts to escape its responsibility for who it is and the choices it makes by assessing the world as imperfect and corrupt and thus essentially mitigating its personal culpability as well as its necessary part in making things right. It is an "after you" mindset.

> The good person out of the good treasure of his heart produces good, and the evil person out of his evil treasure produces evil, for out of the abundance of the heart his mouth speaks. (Luke 6:45)

As a result, this world's corruption, including our individual errors is often conceived as the result of externals which are out of our control. Jesus requires His listeners to accept that their realities, whether good or bad, have their most essential source within each of us and not circumstantially from without. It is this balance of our internal dispositions and their manifestations in our external actions (as words, gestures, choices, etc.) which Jesus is so keen to address and guide. For while circumstantial events are independent of any individual's capacity to control, it is our fundamentally essential aspects of our agency to always be free in determining any events ultimate reality through the meanings we contribute to them. This exposes each of us to the responsibilities that are inescapable and essential to self understanding. It re-focuses us from the givens or the non-chosen facets of our lives to the internally and free choices of the meanings we give to these realities. These meanings often determine "how" we perceive these events and thus "how" we act.

At the deepest spiritual level there is so much wisdom within our spiritual traditions. Generosity of the self is a manifestation of one's capacities to love. Patience with oneself and with others is an acknowledgement of the sacredness of our journey and our need to be humble in our always incomplete understanding of ourselves and our call. This patience with oneself is a prerequisite of our need to circumscribe the often rash judgments we place upon others.

Prayer and meditation are absolute requirements of being open to the mystery of life and our call to be a part of its redemption. Without the ongoing reflection on Jesus' life we are in peril of being disconnected from Him and His messages. This makes apparent the role of discipline in our spiritual lives as the necessary means of keeping our lives imbued with the values, examples and person of Jesus. Integrity which is the openness of one's being to the truth of things and one's self is at the heart of who Jesus is and the message He preached.

In his biography of John Paul II, George Weigel expounds on a realization that came early to the young priest, Karol Wojtyla. It was the realization of the concept of "gift" as central to the right understanding of Christ's lived example of love. What is important about the notion of "gift" both in Wojtyla's ministry and personal theology and to us is that it brings to us the proper orientation of the self in relation to our lives. Weigel explains the young Wojtyla's coming to see that true Christian love is something that both spontaneously emerges in one's awareness as an option which opens the self to perceiving any situation as abounding in possibilities for responding in love. In this way both the startling awareness and the opportunity to respond are understood as the gifts of grace freely offered and requiring a free response. This free offering is thus unconnected to the self's desires or wants. It is essentially the outcome of seeing, knowing and caring for the other. The aspect of knowing that is part of this phenomenon is not merely intellectual. So important was this concept of "gift" to Wojtyla that he often would refer to "the law of the gift" in a similar sense in which one would refer to the "law of nature". In this way the orientation of the person as "gift" is for Wojtyla a primary stance of being open to being given to others as a way of bringing Christ to our broken world.

Knowing is essential as an aspect of this orientation of the person as "gift". In the remarkable work by the renowned philosopher Martha C. Nussbaum entitled "Upheavals of Thought" the author presents a view of knowing that is both rich and pertinent to the view being proposed here. Nussbaum makes explicit the multi-dimensional aspect of knowing, often not fully appreciated in modern western culture. Nussbaum is able to see cognition under two very different, but related lenses. Knowing is the act of a discoverer. It is most appropriately how the academic seeks to engage their objects of inquiry. Knowing is only one method of cognitively embracing the world. Understanding is another dimension of our cognitive capacities. For the purposes of our ongoing reflection, I am going to build on some of the insights of Nussbaum but making a distinction between knowing as intellection and understanding as something far richer.

Understanding is very different than its counterpart knowing. Whereas knowing is an orientation toward mastering that which it seeks to know, understanding is the desire to behold based on our capacity to be receptive and open to what is and what will be. Understanding is thus not grasping and invasive, but receptive and only achieved through dwelling. It is only within this context that the truth of our emotions as being essential additive elements to our complete appreciation of our intellectual capacity can be truly appreciated.

Understanding is comprised of multiple realities; emotions merely establish how we are present to a reality. Understanding also facilitates an appreciation of compassion as an emotion. If it is formulated from a self pre-occupied orientation it can be both paternalistic and diminutive of the dignity of the human person. It is only when compassion and empathy emerge from our non-ego-centric selves or the cognitive grasping associated with knowing as an intellectual endeavor, that they can truly be both expressed and received by another. In this way the concept of "gift" developed by John Paul II can also only proceed from our desire to understand and thus becomes the proper orientation from which we can choose to act.

The kind of knowing that Nussbaum is describing would be much better described as understanding. For knowing is a posture oriented toward grasping its objects and conquering their mysteries. Understanding is more open to the idea of approaching its object with respect and a willingness to experience what one seeks and to meet the objective with less aggressive force. As a result, the concept of dwelling with the object one seeks in order to understand as a method of respectfully allowing it to slowly emerge and reveal its inner secrets is at the heart of understanding. This acceptance of our emotions as being an essential facet of our capacity to understand is the true appreciation of our emotions as having meaningful content to add to our cognitive.

Being aware as an initial step in an orientation to understand and ultimately to respond as gift is a process that must be highly accepting of the dignity and sanctity of the other. Knowing has a very different energy behind it which seeks to conquer the otherness of that which it desires. Knowing is thus an aggressive way of responding to reality. In making these distinctions within our cognitive powers it is important to acknowledge that there are many situations in which knowing is the appropriate orientation, especially in the sciences or in academic pursuits. When it comes to the posture of relating to other people, however, this method does not fit.

For Nussbaum, therefore, the appreciation of our emotions as contributors to our process of knowing can be seen as essential, but somehow lacking, in that the distinction between knowing and understanding has not been achieved. Using the distinction between knowing and understanding, compassion and empathy, which are aspects of understanding, are truly essential to our capacity to embrace life most fully. Both compassion and empathy are results of our desire to understand and in this sense a real aspect of our cognitive powers. For not only must we understand someone's situation to appreciate their suffering, but we must be capable of appreciating the unity of being and thus our inherent connectedness with others, which enables compassion.

As a result of the above reflection another facet of ego-centricity has been revealed and that is the desire to know as the driving force for how one approaches other people. The desire to know others is thus revelatory of a desire to be able to grasp for the purposes of using the other. This stance is thus consistent with the manipulative aspects of ego-centricity. It is a way of assessing others to determine who would be most useful to me. In so doing, I have neither the energy nor the desire to understand them. My first and sole goal is to ascertain who might be able to assist me in achieving the goals or needs that are at the core of my personal energy.

Each above example expresses a cognizance that distortion begins from a distortion within, and ultimately expresses itself in our resulting distorted actions. Each acknowledges the less often stressed truth in Christianity that life and our journey is expressive of the unfolding facet of our becoming which is most completely realized in the acceptance of each individual's unique process of unfolding and the subsequent development of their own individual narrative. It is also an ongoing openness to experience and life such that we can be receptive to God's call in each moment as well as having the capacity to hear our own inner orientation toward ourselves and the other. It should be clear from all that has preceded that this requires an orientation to the self and to others that is deeply respectful of their sanctity and inner mystery. Each individual must be approached via a desire to understand, which is to respect and dwell within the presence of the other; always allowing the other their option to open themselves up to us or not.

In many ways, one has to wonder how this realization might have contributed even more to an understanding of the unique nature of Jesus as both human and divine. In the early patristic period of the Christian faith, the fathers of the early church attempted to clarify Jesus' humanity and divinity in the face of numerous theories that were considered heretical. The truth they wanted to protect was that Jesus was fully human and divine simultaneously. The problem was that these men had been significantly influenced by Platonic thought and therefore

THE WAY OF SERVICE

accepted that humanity and divinity were vastly different realities that were appreciated as almost antithetical. Until the advent of Aquinas this problem remained hidden in the complex language of the patristic period and carried forth in the later teaching of St. Augustine. Thomas Aquinas did not accept the presupposition that to be human and to be divine were radically different realities. In fact Aquinas saw humanity as being the potential for divinity. Aquinas accepted the human will as the determiner of our capacity to achieve our fullness through the proper aligning of our wills to that of the Father. Thus, Jesus' reality as human and divine were not in contradiction or internal antagonism, but existed as potential to actual. Only via Jesus' will could these two aspects of His single nature be integrated. This view of Jesus as most fully human and in this way divine now coupled with an appreciation that His identity and self understanding were the result of a continuous process of unfolding and openness as well as a basic orientation of Himself as gift adds significant dimensions to our appreciation of who He was and how He was. It also stands as the paradigm of our potential and call.

Jesus, like us, was a dynamic process of unfolding and self realization. Jesus, like us, was continuously confronted by the choice to embrace His ongoing unfolding and thus essential mystery. He was also always presented with the option of taking the time to understand those who came to him or to briskly assess and dismiss. As a fellow human, Jesus only fully grasped His divinity and purpose as they revealed themselves to him in time. This reality exposes the depth of the very real call given to each of us, His followers, to embrace with faith our vulnerable realities as well as our need to continually be open to our ongoing revelation of who we are and who we are being called to be.

The role of the distorted ego is also an essential element in understanding the complete appreciation of suffering as a very real aspect of human existence. The distorted ego is certainly not the sole source of our experience of suffering. It is, however, a significant contributor to the quality of our suffering. Suffering is essentially our being passive to and unable to control reality. It is the natural outgrowth of our natures as beings that must learn to effectively deal with the infinity of "givens", which are essential aspects of our lives.

Our desperate clawing desire to control life is a source of genuine suffering. The ongoing experience that most of the events that fill our lives are beyond our control has not facilitated humanity's acceptance of this truth. The simple fact that life is filled with an infinite number of events that we are not capable of determining and the reality that suffering is a necessary and integral part of life are very difficult realities to accept. What our ego-distortion adds to this suffering is the underlying belief that suffering is not a necessary part of human reality and that we can or should be able to eradicate suffering from our lives. This is another of the lies that seeks to permeate human reality. While desiring suffering is not what is being promulgated, neither is a denial of the very real and often tragic dimensions of suffering. The truth that stands in opposition to the lie that we should not have to suffer is the fact that suffering is an essential part of human experience.

The suffering associated with loss is one of the givens of life and is often enlarged by the erroneous expectation that I should not have to lose; the experience of suffering due to change is the result of the bizarre notion that life should not bring change. This in no manner mitigates the truth that loss and physical pain are quite real and not the result of any distortion. What is often the cause of increased suffering or, in fact, suffering itself can be our projection into the future of that which has not yet occurred or our ability to dwell on a past that was equally painful yet no longer exists. Another cause of suffering can also be our inability to grasp one of life's events in a manner which allows one to accept this suffering as part of our human journey and the reality that suffering plays in this journey.

Death of a loved one is a very poignant example of true suffering on behalf of those who mourn the deceased. The central point of this portion of our reflection is not on the validity of suffering itself. It is rather a discussion of the various ways humans can add to suffering through our distorted expectations, our capacity to project scenarios into a future yet to be revealed as a method of control as well as the ways we internalize suffering and make sense of it. The meanings we impose on certain events can increase our sorrow and pain because they cannot see an event in life within the larger context of our life experience and faith.

The suffering associated with death coupled with an orientation toward death as not the natural progression of our life and our continued unfolding through the inevitable stripping away of the unnecessary, or in the case of a loved one, the stripping away of attachments as a real facet of life's process. In fact, it is the reality of suffering and its textures and its place within the process of coming into being that is an essential aspect of human life that can catch one up short if one has not been attuned to the seasons of one's life and of those one cares for. Once one can accept suffering as well as the underlying reality that one cannot control much of life, but must allow one's self to be carried by its current, only then can the reality of suffering be ensured of its proper depth and boundaries for it is not encumbered with additional erroneous weights.

The ever present truth of life's flowing and our being in process necessitates that we must embrace the trustful posture of the journeyer who must let go of the present to make space for the next instance. It can only be embraced by one dispassionate, detached and deeply believing in the wonder and mystery, awe and sacredness of each infinite now which unfolds as the very substance of life. For as it says in the New Testament:

> So don't worry about tomorrow, for tomorrow will bring its own worries. Today's trouble is enough for today. (Matthew 6:34)

The above allusion concerning the reality of worry is at the heart of a life lived in distortion. Worry results from our desire to control what is impossible to control. It is the result of not having faith that I am truly loved and thus a firm acceptance that I will be cared for and that the manner in which life unfolds will not overcome me. Worry is based on our capacity to develop various scenarios for the future. Often worriers create scenarios that are the most bleak and frightening because through projecting these various options on the future they believe they can best prepare themselves for outcomes not determined or necessary. As Jesus notes, another aspect of a distorted human life is our inability to live in the moment. For Jesus this capacity requires faith and trust in God and the reality that each of us is loved and cared for as individuals. Without this there is little capacity to allow life to unfold without our need to control through worry or manipulation. How much unnecessary human suffering is the outcome of not being able to enjoy the moment, when our stomachs are full and those we love are around us, due to the fact that many are already postulating multiple scenarios for what is yet to come, as if by so doing we could change any of them.

As a result of the development of the understanding of ego distortion and the true nature of each person as a unique journeyer on their individual path one should now be able to comprehend three dimensions of truth. To truly perceive ourselves and all reality as they are in themselves is to understand them as expressing the ongoing coming into being and passing away of all reality. To perceive things as other than having these attributes is to deceive oneself and is expressive of an erroneous orientation to truth. Much of our suffering results from our not truly accepting that everything, even ourselves, is undergoing constant change and that there is no static "I" that somehow escapes this reality. What often confuses us into believing in the static 'I" is that the flow of experiences that is part of our existence mistakenly implies a subject that precedes and remains after one experience flows into another. While certainly there is some residual trace of the past that remains and influences our future it is not determinate.

Once we postulate this concrete self we find that suffering increases as we grasp those experiences that bring joy and suffer their impermanence. This does not mean that our capacity to freely give meaning to ourselves and our experiences is a mistake. It merely makes explicit that the self, whom we attempt to postulate and cling to is not required of the life that participates in its process of living. We must come to accept ourselves as coming into being and fading away as the notes in a symphony.

Few of us would deny the fact that the Fifth Symphony of Beethoven is really the insubstantial notes, transitory as they are, which comprise the beauty that is itself made up of the ongoing coming into being and going away of each note. Few of us would not understand the absurdity of trying to hold onto one of these notes, no matter how beautiful, and thereby not allowing the fullness of the whole to complete. All the same, these notes as they come into being and fade away produce a reality of unquestioned beauty, in and of necessity resulting from their ephemeral passing. These truths are put forward in the hard language of Jesus:

> If any of you wants to be my follower, you must turn from your selfish ways, take up your cross, and follow me. If you try to hang on to your life, you will lose it. But if you give up your life for my sake and for the sake of the Good News, you will save it. And what do you benefit if you gain the whole world but lose your own soul? Is anything worth more than your soul? If anyone is ashamed of me and my message in these adulterous and sinful days, the Son of Man will be ashamed of that person when he returns in the glory of his Father with the holy angels. (Mark 8:34-38)

In the life of Jesus it is not merely in quotations such as above that His view of the right orientation of the individual to things, societal honor, suffering and self giving are exposed, but in his very life as a tour de force. For it is in appreciating His orientation toward material things, human comforts as well as the views of those around him who were in power and considered important, where Jesus' true detachment was manifest. It is also in His ongoing willingness to embrace the simplicity of a detached life where we can truly see His lived appreciation for what and who is important. Most importantly it is also in His free journey to Jerusalem and to the ignominy of His death that Jesus makes clear His lived acceptance of impermanence and love. While Jesus says very little about the role of suffering in life, He lives a message that clearly says that suffering gets its meaning and power from the one who suffers. Jesus' faith in His Father and in His being loved completely enable Him to bear suffering in a manner very different from one who can only see in it its meaninglessness and its apparent injustice in taking its residence in his person or house.

Another reality that should reinforce this spirituality, especially as it relates to the question of the ego can be found in the Jewish notion of God espoused in the Hebrew Scriptures and in whose image we were clearly created as potentials. God's manifestation of Himself is both rare and filled with mystery. He first showed Himself to Moses as a burning bush.

Now Moses was keeping the flock of his father-in-law, Jethro the priest of Midian; and he led his flock to the west side of the wilderness, and came to Horeb, the mountain of God. And the angel of the Lord appeared to him in a flame of fire out of the middle out of the midst of a bush; and he looked, and lo, the bush was burning, yet it was not consumed. And Moses said "I will turn aside and see this great sight, why the bush is not burnt." When the Lord saw that he turned aside to see, God called to him out of the bush, "Moses, Moses!" And he said, "Here am I" Then he said "Do not come near; put off your shoes from your feet, for the place on which you are standing is holy ground." And he said, "I am the God of your father, the God of Abraham, the God of Isaac, and the God of Jacob." (Genesis 3: 1-6)

Here we have God manifesting himself as the fire that both is and is not. In another text, when Moses asks God His name, God responds "I am who am" (Genesis 3:14). This moniker is an identification of God as pure love which is being without limit. For God does not exist as a Sam, or Martha or as any other thing, He is pure love, which is unlimited being, which is pouring itself forth in its eternal renewal. We who are made to be in His image through the right functioning of our wills are thus not made in the image of an encapsulated deity. By extension, our understanding of ourselves as unfolding processes and not static egos is in line with our call to be *ad imago Dei* or potential images of God.

For each human being is life, as is the creator, and each human life is created such that it is enabled to express itself; or in less technical terms, it will give its life away in the ongoing act of love. While the Greeks worshiped (in a manner of speaking) "Being" itself, Christians were to discover that the Greek notion of "Being" as the ultimate reality was nothing if it could not give expression to its superabundance of existence. Thus the concept of the "Word" articulated in the prologue of the Gospel of St. John married the notion of Supreme Being and its expression as one and the same reality. In Christian terminology this would cement the relationship between the Father, pure being, and the Son, the Logos of the Father. Only later would this essentially Platonic view of God and the Son come to be understood as bringing forth the Holy Spirit (or *anima*) as the life emanating force, which gives expression to all creation, especially the creation of the human person.

Later in the Book of Kings, when God comes before his frustrated Prophet Elijah, he again expresses His identity as the animating breath that made clay into the first man, but this time as expressed in the gentlest almost imperceptible breeze which is never static as it comes from, we know not where and proceeds to an equally mysterious place. (1Kings 19: 9-16)

We live in a time in which the distorted ego appears to be prominent in western culture. This truth is expressed in the heightened materialism that threatens the economic stability of our culture. It is the very center of our capitalism, our incredible marketing machine which seems incapable of being silenced. It manifests its tragic distortions in the all-to-many deaths of our children in acts of killing only to posses the victim's sneakers or jacket. It has most recently exposed itself in the un-tempered greed of many of our CEOs who have used many long standing companies as the means to line their own pockets with more money than one can fathom needing in a lifetime. The disposition of the ego is also perceived in the all-too apparent presence of those without essential means who crouch in church doorways or upon grates with warm air flowing from them as their only means of warmth. It is both their presence in this land of abundance as well as the unfathomable lack of notice by the many individuals who pass by them that gives expression to our lived distortions.

As we move forward in discussing the inauthentic path of *non-serviam*, it will become apparent that it is most essentially an expression of ego distortion. As we will discover, both *non-serviam* and *serviam* while expressing specific "ways", which each of us is able to choose to follow, will also take on unique characteristics that will give expression to the unique individuals each of us are. As a result, while each of the descriptions of the specific ways will have generalized characterizations they will also be capable of nuanced manifestations that are the result of our unique individual natures.

CHAPTER 3

Introduction—*Non-serviam*

"*Non-serviam*" or the choice to live a journey in which one will not serve sounds so very blatant, so very bold. One might even think that the very concept is in fact ludicrous. First, who would ever sit down and decide to live this kind of life? The very sound of it is brash and unbecoming. Unfortunately, while these perceptions may be true, it is equally true that "*Non-serviam*" is more prevalent than many would realize or wish to accept. Albeit, few of the individuals well ensconced on this path would probably be as self aware as to note it and then even less likely to name it as such. It is, in many respects, the subtlety of this "Way" that makes it so very dangerous and so much more a part of our culture than one would imagine.

What makes the articulation of this way significant to any person serious about the quality of their life as well as their desire to follow in the path of Jesus is that it exposes the core of both Jesus' message and our numerous methods for deviating from it. As distinguished from the traditional moral discussions, a moral framework based on the description of the following of "Ways" is not focused on human "acts" per se, as the best moral indicator rather it is emphasizing the predispositions that make these actions often inevitable.

This moral framework based on the ancient concept of "ways" is particularly true to the messages and life of Jesus of

Nazareth. If one reads the Gospels one of the elements that seems particularly and almost glaringly missing is the usual lists of laws to guide one's actions. In the case of Jesus' life and teachings this lack of specific moral precepts and moral avoidances is consistent with Jesus' fundamental belief that one's character is revealed and developed from within. As always, the balance to this being the acknowledgement of the fact that after many of His teachings, which focused on one's interior orientations Jesus was fond of saying, "Go, and do the same." thus His call was clearly for us to follow in our actions not merely in our intentions. For this reason the internal dispositions of the human person were of utmost concern to Him—not merely our actions, however. Jesus was all too familiar with those for whom their faith hung on them like the cloths they wore. In this sense one's faith was something to be observed by others. Jesus knew how prevalent were those that played the role of the religious person or the man of God, but whose internal dispositions were as far from the truths of their faith as they could be.

In the same way, Jesus believed and taught that each human being was a unique manifestation of the Father and thus a sacred being. This also entailed a refocusing of our human sensibilities from the external impressions which we immediately perceive to being open to discovering who someone truly is through a more in-depth engagement with them. This critical orientation is essential to grasp for those of us living in the modern western culture since our culture has evolved in exactly the opposite way. We spend countless amounts of money on our external appearances. We often make almost immediate judgments about others based on their appearances and our attraction to or repulsion from one another. The often sad effect is that many very interesting people are not discovered and far too many vacuous people get central billing.

Jesus' way of looking at morality is based on the dignity and wonder of the human person. As a result it both entails a discussion of the individual as well as the larger community as inextricably bound realities. After reflecting on what shall be presented, the reader is thus less likely to come away with the marked clarity which resulted from legalistic approaches to morality. Instead, one will now be able to both understand and assess one's life from a deeper appreciation of the vocation offered to each of us and the implications of our free choices on who we are and the world in which we live.

A not so subtle indicator of a *non-serviam* orientation is a preoccupation with self, which obscures reality and the decisions that reveal one's values and perspectives. When my needs, my future and my dreams reside at the core of my being they have a very powerful sway over what I can see or feel. In this way they profoundly sway what is considered important.

> Then Jesus told his disciples, "If any man would come after me, let him deny himself and take up his cross and follow me. For whoever would save his life will lose it, and whoever loses his life for my sake will find it. For what will it profit a man, if he gains the whole world and forfeits his life? Or what shall a man give in return for his life? For the Son of man is to come with his angels in the glory of his Father, and then he will repay every man for what he has done. (Matthew 16: 24-28)

From this passage from the gospel of St. Matthew it is made explicit that the way to find one's self is through giving that self away. The way of following Jesus is not a path away from suffering. The necessity of accepting the crosses that will be given to one as a part of one's life are an essential facet of our Christian faith. The lived life of Jesus is a warning that those who spend inordinate amounts of energy and emotional concern on "saving their lives" or focused on acquiring material things or on living for the esteem of others, or for acquiring power and prestige are ensconced on paths of dissipation.

The young corporate manager, preoccupied with his or her advancing career so that he or she can provide for his or her growing family, is not evil or worthy of our distain. Over time, the question will be whether this young man or woman can recognize when he or she has secured enough corporate success? Will he or she notice when the material benefits of success have reached the level where any more would be unnecessary or at too great a cost to the other valued elements of their life.

This initial distortion is a natural progression that many have followed and which has been able to catch more than a few in its alluring promises. Success, in human terms, can and is often one of the most alluring paths able to beckon one to follow. It is not the things in themselves nor is it the success per se that is the core of the entrapment. It is the slow emergence of self preoccupation, a kind of narcissism, more familiar with infantile development, which often begins as a normal desire to succeed and based on one's larger concerns to be responsible for the others in one's life. What is essential is that we not forget what is truly important.

Do not store up for yourselves treasures on earth, where moth and rust destroy, and where thieves break in and steal. But store up for yourselves treasures in heaven, where moth and rust do not destroy, and where thieves do not break in and steal. For where your treasure is, there your heart will be also. (Matthew 6:19-21)

When this focus is no longer on one's loved ones, rather on one's personal self preoccupation then one can be almost sure that one is on the wrong path.

It is at this point where one can truly loose one's sense of oneself and as a result turn to things and the admiration of others to provide what was once clearly understood and expressive of one's cherished values. It is at this point that an internal struggle can begin to gnaw at one's self. Initially, the objectives behind the hard work, which brought recognition, were clearly the desire to provide for those one loves. In fact, it was this fuel that enabled one to put increasing levels of one's heart and soul into one's work. Somewhere along the way, this source of one's effort shifted and the objective was no longer just ensuring a comfortable home for one's family. Now the many nights away from those one loves and the ability to make more and more of the things so important to them begins to reveal something else driving one's apparent unfettered success.

From the above example it is clear that one of the most visible signs of a *non-serviam* "way" of being is a self, preoccupied with one's own desires and needs. This self centeredness is the result of a distortion which minimizes one's capacity to perceive one's life from a complete perspective.

The self who is now the center of one's concern results in a lack of appreciation for how certain actions, words or decisions might affect those for whom one ought to be more concerned. This tunnel vision can be very subtle in its coming into being. It often results from very common and seemingly innocent decisions, but can very easily cause one to be swept up by self preoccupation.

It is our natural desire to be appreciated by others. It is quite another thing when one begins to let others define them. Everyone desires to be held in high esteem as individuals and in one's work as well as in the many varied roles that one comes to play in the normal course of life. The distortion begins when our successes and their accompanying praise and varied accolades begin to be the basis for our sense of who we are. This means that we have begun to allow ourselves to be defined by external messages or things. It is this externalization of the self that is ultimately ruinous. Jesus' teaching about the meaning of living life to its fullest and the right values associated with right living are very illustrative.

> If any man would come after me, let him deny himself, and take up his cross, and follow me. For whosoever would save his life shall lose it; and whosoever shall lose his life for my sake and the gospel's shall save it. For what doth it profit a man, to gain the whole world, and forfeit his life? For what should a man give in exchange for his life? (Mark 8: 34-38)

The core questions concerning life and the choices each of us will face are placed before us in the above quote. These words stand in stark contrast to much of what our culture emphasizes and presents to our children. It is strange that Jesus sets up the loss of one's life, the denial of self and the juxtaposition of gaining the whole world and the forfeiting of one's life. Wouldn't most modern people pause over this? For don't most of us believe that gaining the whole world would be gaining life to its fullest? Who among us believes that the essentials to the fullness of life are in self denial, accepting one's cross (or sufferings), or in giving one's life away? If one had to guess—it would be few of us. What, therefore is awry?

We live in a culture where the optimal event for most of us would be winning the lottery. We live in a culture that says why deny oneself? We have credit for getting those things we cannot afford and which many of us believe we deserve. As for accepting one's cross, how many of us do not take every opportunity to bemoan our sufferings. How many of us turn to pharmaceuticals to solve life's issues. Even fewer of us end our days asking whether we were open to perceiving anyone in need no less responding to them as a way of giving our lives away. For many of us for whom the above is true, it is not too late. Our die has not been cast. We must, however think about this small quote and the lives we choose to live and honestly reconcile who we may think we are and who we may think inspires our lives and then face the reality.

As a result of the natural progression of many a person's life, one begins to shed many aspects of one's life and to focus on that which now brings this needed recognition. The reason for this drastic shift is most often the result of the fact that one has become dependent for their sense of themselves on these external messages. The internal values of our past, which we developed over time and from which our self emerged are now giving way to different values. At the same time as one is allowing one's self to be defined by things and people, I begin to lose the natural perspective that was once mine. The more I succeed the more my focus and energy are spent in maintaining the lauds and favor of those whose notice is deemed most important. Soon significant amounts of my energy and time are shifted to that which has become my focus and away from the larger concerns of my life. How often individuals who have been victims of this process have noted that their happiest years were when they had nothing, but their small family and a position that was anything but glorious and which provided just enough.

The distortion of allowing oneself to be defined by others is both serious and very hard to correct. Once my "self" identity is tied to the ever changing and fickle opinions of others, I become addicted to their lauds and signs of respect. In my blindness, I often allow the many other important aspects of my life to wither without my attention and focus. This loss of my very self is a most pernicious manifestation of a *non-serviam* way of existence. As a distortion it is a manifestation of the fact that what I am truly sensitive to and focused upon are my own successes and the accompanying adulations and advancements. Many a family has been ruined and divided due to this particular path. One can recognize oneself as caught in this snare if one finds themselves pining and preoccupied about advancement at work, and the constant need for affirmation from others.

Having been told of my inherent worth by others and having accepted the symbols of this success, it is not uncommon for the individual to accept a further distortion. I begin to truly see myself as different from others, and as such my scope of concern, generosity and self giving continue to narrow. I may even begin to develop a distain for those who have not progressed as I have. For I was able to get where I am through hard work and thus their lack of success must be due to either laziness or a lack of quickness of mind.

Soon all the symbols of my success such as the size of my home and the beautiful things that I have filled it with become both an anchor that keeps me focused and a weight that bares me down. For they are the trappings which make who I am visible to others and externally express my being part of the community of those who have made it. As my success continues, so often do the acquisitions of externals, the material expressions of who I am. This often entails a larger home, a more prestigious car, potentially a summer home and trips to exotic places.

The real issue must remain clear. It is not the things per se. It is not the success. It is the loss of my "self" and the forgetting of what is essential that is truly the issue. It is also the self absorption and the narrowing of my natural concerns for others, which expresses my distortions. At its core, of all these aspects of my *non-serviam* life are the result of my allowing myself to be defined by external praise and the material acquisitions that are now how I perceive myself.

Jesus, full of the Holy Spirit, returned from the Jordan and was led by the Spirit in the desert, where for forty days he was tempted by the devil. He ate nothing during those days, and at the end of them he was hungry. The devil said to him, "If you are the Son of God, tell this stone to become bread." Jesus answered, "It is written: 'Man does not live on bread alone.'" The devil led him up to a high place and showed him in an instant all the kingdoms of the world. And he said to him, "I will give you all their authority and splendor, for it has been given to me, and I can give it to anyone I want to. So if you worship me, it will all be yours." Jesus answered, "It is written: 'Worship the Lord your God and serve him only.'" The devil led him to Jerusalem and had him stand on the highest point of the temple. "If you are the Son of God," he said, "throw yourself down from here. For it is written:" 'He will command his angels concerning you to guard you carefully; they will lift you up in their hands, so that you will not strike your foot against a stone.' "Jesus answered, "It says: 'Do not put the Lord your God to the test.'" When the devil had finished all this tempting, he left him until an opportune time. (Luke 4: 1-13)

This very familiar part of the Gospels is often lost on many of us who have practiced our faith for many years. We have heard it all so many times. Let us spend but a few moments with this piece of the life of Jesus once more. Jesus has just been baptized by John in the Jordon. This is a baptism of repentance and associated with the awaiting of the Chosen One. Immediately after His baptism, Jesus goes out alone into the desert. While certainly this may be factual, it is also very richly spiritual.

Jesus has reached an age where he must face the existential emptiness that John of the Cross called "the dark night of the soul." Many of us have an experience in our lives where we too have come face to face with our deserts. During these times food lacks its taste and life seems endlessly empty. The devil joins Jesus here for it is at this time that his lies can have the greatest impact. For one who is hungry food is the answer. For one who seeks power, recognition and the envy of one's friends the lie of having it all is offered. For anyone who is suffering it is the offer of being made well. The lie, however, is not necessarily in not being given what one asks for, but in the hope that the desert will become an oasis through the fulfillment of one's wish.

At its most basic, all of this is the outcome of our acceptance of the greatest lie. It is a lie which from the beginning promised the very thing that each person who walks this earth has desperately sought to believe and that is that there is a difference between one human being and another. It is the desire to believe that there can be a greatest angel, a most perfect ruler or more to the point the desire to believe that who I am is somehow special and more worthy of the many wonders this world has to offer. It is in part behind our insatiable desire to be the most beautiful, the most intelligent or the most skilled. It is that which feeds our beauty centered culture. It is the foundation of our youth obsessed societies. In this way it is the very arrogance that has always been behind the penultimate sin.

It is the convoluted desire to be above all other creatures and in this sense to be like God. This warped illusion is the lie of lies. It sets up the deluded into believing that only he or she is worthy of service, of being seen, understood and ultimately loved. Part of this lie is also a fundamental need to abrogate death, change and our need for authentic relationships. It postulates the capacity to cheat life by winning or, perhaps better put, by beating everyone else as the symbol of the truth which I am attempting to fabricate about who I am.

Like Icarus of Greek mythology, it is the ecstasy experienced through the capacity to seem like a god that causes one to dare to fly too close to the truth, the sun, and which ultimately brings one crashing back into reality.

Daedalus (who had been consigned to the labyrinth of Crete for offenses against the gods) conceived to escape from the Labyrinth with his son, Icarus, from Crete by constructing wings and then flying to safety. He built the wings from feathers and wax, and before the two set off he warned Icarus not to fly too low lest his wings touch the waves and get wet and not too high lest the sun melt the wax. But the young Icarus, overwhelmed by the thrill of flying, did not heed his father's warning, and flew too close to the sun whereupon the wax in his wings melted and he fell into the sea.

Another fundamental lie of *non-serviam* is that I can control reality. In some cases this is a further belief in one's individual power to control, resulting from what one has achieved through talent, manipulation, amassed resources and often the use of others as mere pawns in one's clawing to the top. Wealth has always brought with it the capacity to have the best that this world can offer. In many respects this wealth can appear to give one mastery and control over many of life's benefits, delights and capabilities. Whether this means being able to gain access to other powerful people, or the capacity to get my children into the most prestigious schools, my capacity to get to the head of important lines, and to have access where access is limited, it can appear from the perspective of ordinary people that indeed the affluent do have the capacity to control much of life. When, however, one looks closely at the real aspects of life such as one's relationships, sickness, death, natural disasters and the normal losses that are parts of every person's existence, these apparent levers of control quickly show their feebleness.

Jesus saw these distortions as a significant encumbrance on *The Way of Service*, He was espousing. In the Gospel of St. Matthew, Jesus makes a statement that has puzzled many for generations,

> Again I say to you, it is easier for a camel to go through the eye of a needle, than for a rich man to enter the kingdom of God. (Matthew 19:24)

The meaning behind this short, but very powerful proclamation has little necessary connection to actual money or gold. It does have everything to do with those who perceive themselves as having enough. The concept of being rich, which is being played with by Jesus is meant to delineate those who believe they are complete, ultimately satisfied and in little need of others. It is an orientation that denies our existential incompleteness, which is an essential part of our human condition. It is the lie that proclaims that I need no one, not even God. It is the denial of the Psalmists prayer,

> As a hart longs for flowing streams, so longs my soul for thee, O God. My soul thirsts for God, for the living God. When shall I come and behold the face of God? (Psalm 42: 1-2)

It is also the denial of the profound insight espoused by St. Augustine of Hippo in his Confessions when he repeats in his own way the truth of the psalmist just quoted.

Almighty God,
you have made us for yourself,
and our hearts are restless
till they find their rest in you;

It is this sense of being complete in and of myself that Jesus rightly proclaims will keep us from entering the kingdom of God. For this sense of satiation is really the ultimate poverty associated with embracing the lie that we are not creatures and reaching the realization that true fulfillment can never be ours in this life. It is the truth of the simple age old image of the glass full of liquid that thus cannot accept any more. In this sense, it is a lack of openness or a capacity to accept anything that this glass symbolizes. For this reason not even God, who desires for us to be receptive to his ongoing calls to truth, will try to force more where more is not needed or where it cannot be accepted.

Many with significant means have been able to distance themselves from their own wealth and thus making themselves objects of this warning. Material wealth does not of necessity place one in the condition we have been describing. Many persons with means have not defined themselves by what they have and continue to see, hear, and respond to the needy through more than mere check writing. In the same way that poverty does not necessitate sanctity, neither does wealth guarantee shallowness, self preoccupation nor a lack of capacity to either see, hear or respond to the needy.

The person who lives always conscious of the adage "There, but for the grace of God, go I." is accepting one's place in life. It is the acceptance that I have no claim to my life or my lifestyle that is being called for. It is the acceptance that every gift, whether of mind or body or the family I was born into, is a gift always capable of being lost or taken away. As a gift it is not earned, but given. As such, the gift can be taken away through no fault of the individual. The scenario of one's life can be fundamentally altered and not due to one's sin. For this gift was initially one's gift of life from the God who created each of us. Once born, each human person is part of the natural laws of change that govern this world. Certainly, the kind of person we are can have either a positive or negative effect on the flow of our lives. Regardless, significant elements of our lives will be the results of the natural unfolding of events that are part of our life, which has no regard for station, prominence or success. Whatever the case, what unfolds in life is often neither caused by us nor the result of a vindictive deity.

Now there were some present at that time who told Jesus about the Galileans whose blood Pilate had mixed with their sacrifices. Jesus answered, "Do you think that these Galileans were worse sinners than all the other Galileans because they suffered this way? I tell you, no! But unless you repent, you too will all perish. Or those eighteen who died when the tower in Siloam fell on them—do you think they were more guilty than all the others living in Jerusalem? I tell you, no! But unless you repent, you too will all perish."

Then he told this parable: "A man had a fig tree, planted in his vineyard, and he went to look for fruit on it, but did not find any. So he said to the man who took care of the vineyard, 'For three years now I've been coming to look for fruit on this fig tree and haven't found any. Cut it down! Why should it use up the soil?'

'Sir,' the man replied, 'leave it alone for one more year, and I'll dig around it and fertilize it. If it bears fruit next year, fine! If not, then cut it down.' (Luke 13: 1-9)

It is this realization which each of us must come to accept that often overcomes us with fear. This fear and its companion, despair are often the basis for many of the distortions we have been describing. Each of us must face our existential vulnerability. Attempting to rid life of this truth will only bring more sorrow. Facing our most basic fears requires faith. It requires faith in God and faith in who we are and more essentially a faith in each other. For no individual can face the realities of existence alone. It is another facet of the distortion of *non-serviam,* which states that we do not need each other. It is an arrogance that claims I can face life as a rugged individual. I can face the existential terror of death through my own inner strength. These lies corrode our communities. They dilute our capacities to love and be loved. They are the source of many of our distortions.

In periods of suffering the value of the community can take its most apparent form. For it is only through sharing one's sorrows and one's fears that we can truly come to accept our inherent vulnerability. The truth of our humanity as essentially communal is something that has been weakened by our modern mobile society. This reality does not mitigate our need for community, but makes the creation and sustaining of community all the more difficult. Community remains an essential aspect of healthy human living. It begins with the smallest community of the family, but it does and cannot end there. It is essential that humans gain a new appreciation of the necessity of the larger community and develop ways to make this a reality in a world in which significant portions of the population move from one place to another. Without real community our rituals and our lives are drained of much of the richness they seek to express. Without real community and mutual concern and support, the vulnerabilities of life can become overwhelming.

Jesus focused much of His teaching on the requirement of accepting our incomplete natures and our need to embrace and to live with this realization. This inner openness carved out of us through suffering and our acceptance that life is not ours to control is an essential aspect of the orientation open to God's love and Word. This was most magnificently represented in the famous Sermon on the Mount.

Now when he saw the crowds, he went up on a mountainside and sat down. His disciples came to him, and he began to teach them saying:

"Blessed are the poor in spirit, for theirs is the kingdom of heaven.
Blessed are those who mourn,
for they will be comforted.
Blessed are the meek,
for they will inherit the earth.
Blessed are those who hunger and thirst for righteousness,
for they will be filled.
Blessed are the merciful,
for they will be shown mercy.
Blessed are the pure in heart,
for they will see God.
Blessed are the peacemakers,
for they will be called sons of God.
Blessed are those who are persecuted because of righteousness, for theirs is the kingdom of heaven.

Blessed are you when people insult you, persecute you and falsely say all kinds of evil against you because of me. Rejoice and be glad, because great is your reward in heaven, for in the same way they persecuted the prophets who were before you. (Matthew 5: 1-12)

Certainly, Jesus is not espousing a masochism which seeks suffering; rather He is powerfully turning the values of this world upside down. The blessed, pointed out by Jesus, are those who are incomplete and thus the lowly of this earth. They are those who mourn, who are poor in spirit and those who are open to those who need. God is giving His prominence to those who respond with generosity, mercy and love. This inverted set of values points out those who have little and yet are willing to share the little they have. It is also the vocation of those with much to discern the true value of their excess in light of those who need. It demands of us who have a detachment that enables us to give to those without.

These blessed are not somehow impervious to their situations as if they could be numb to the realities of what life has laid before them. Their blessedness is the result of their capacity to accept what life has dealt them with a more complete understanding of their capacity to see beyond the immediate suffering and never let go of a hope and faith that makes each tomorrow gleam with possibilities. It is based on the humble acceptance that we cannot change that which life places before us. We cannot somehow escape the flow of life, which brings both joy and sorrow. It is also the outcome of a faith in ourselves as well as the realization that somewhere there is a person whose suffering even exceeds mine. I am in no way trying to suggest, however, that every needy person is imbued with sanctity due to their need. Their being blessed in

Jesus' eyes is not a result of their moral rectitude, rather the effect of their existential need and lowliness. Certainly, if a specific individual in this state decides to embrace a life of crime to escape this condition it would no longer be true to say that they were really one of those Jesus was describing as having the conditions of the "blessed"

Meditating on the New Testament for further indicators of a *non-serviam* orientation, is most informative when standing back from the details in order to listen to the quality of the interactions at the core of Jesus' dialogues and sermons. As a fellow Jew, Jesus is passionate and deeply concerned that His faith is true to the message of His Father. Jesus desperately wanted Judaism to be the source of comfort, love and hope for all those who looked to it as their faith. From this perspective, Jesus' ongoing dialogue with many of the leaders of the Jewish community at that time was one of challenge. The challenge was not from the position of one standing outside of the faith community and looking in, but as one from within the community of believers. Jesus was a man of incredible faith and as such a Jewish man crying out for its leaders to remember who they were and who they were called to be. Often the examples of *non-serviam* are represented by the Jewish leaders and the law that they had interpreted in such a way as to protect themselves from the very essence of their faith.

On one occasion, Jesus and His disciples were walking through a wheat field and His disciples were plucking the heads of the wheat. Jesus was confronted by the Jewish leaders, for as a teacher He had to know that this activity violated the Sabbath laws. As a result of this and many other confrontations, Jesus clarifies His beliefs about the centrality of Jewish law in a manner that has left many confused.

Do not think that I have come to abolish the Law or the Prophets; I have not come to abolish them but to fulfill them. I tell you the truth, until heaven and earth disappear, not the smallest letter, not the least stroke of a pen, will by any means disappear from the Law until everything is accomplished. Anyone who breaks one of the least of these commandments and teaches others to do the same will be called least in the kingdom of heaven, but whoever practices and teaches these commands will be called great in the kingdom of heaven. For I tell you that unless your righteousness surpasses that of the Pharisees and the teachers of the law, you will certainly not enter the kingdom of heaven.(Matthew 5:17-21)

In this statement Jesus is making clear the distinction between the manner in which the law is being interpreted by the Jewish leaders of His day and the truth of the law if correctly understood and lived. After making this statement, Jesus clarified His meaning through the juxtaposition of the law as it was usually interpreted and the manner in which He saw it. In this set of juxtaposed views Jesus focuses on five central teachings of the law: lust, divorce, the making of oaths, retaliation and love.

You have heard that it was said, 'You shall not commit adultery. 'But I say to you that everyone who looks at a woman with lustful intent has already committed adultery with her in his heart...
Again you have heard that it was said to those of old, 'You shall not swear falsely, but shall perform to the Lord what you have sworn.' But I say to you, Do not take an oath at all, either by heaven, for it is the throne

of God, or by the earth, for it is his footstool, or by Jerusalem, for it is the city of the great King. And do not take an oath by your head, for you cannot make one hair white or black. Let what you say be simply 'Yes' or 'No'; anything more than this comes from evil.

You have heard that it was said, 'An eye for an eye and a tooth for a tooth. 'But I say to you, do not resist the one who is evil. But if anyone slaps you on the right cheek, turn to him the other also. And if anyone would sue you and take your tunic let him have your cloak as well. And if anyone forces you to go one mile, go with him two miles. Give to the one who begs from you, and do not refuse the one who would borrow from you.

You have heard that it was said, 'You shall love your neighbor and hate your enemy.' But I say to you, Love your enemies and pray for those who persecute you, so that you may be sons of your Father who is in heaven. For he makes his sun rise on the evil and on the good and sends rain on the just and on the unjust. For if you love those who love you, what reward do you have? Do not even the tax collectors do the same? And if you greet only your brothers, what more are you doing than others? Do not even the Gentiles do the same? You therefore must be perfect, as your heavenly Father is perfect.(Matthew 5:27-29, 31-48)

Jesus sets up the sermon by articulating inauthentic interpretations of the law by contemporary religious authorities. In the first example, Jesus does not criticize the law's concern for adultery, but focuses on the existential reality that actions such as adultery are most often the last act in a series of much smaller, but very important choices. The final act of adultery itself is but the almost necessary outcome of a set of decisions starting from how one looks at another to the choice of continued fascination through the numerous steps that one freely chooses long before the act itself. By highlighting the reality of one's internal disposition as the seed of evil, Jesus is targeting the essence of the sin and not merely specific acts that might have been identified as such in the past. It is essential that each member of any community cherish the subjective wonder, mystery and importance in which each of us is held by God. By appreciating ourselves as children of God, and at the same time appreciating other people as of equal stature, our ways of seeing, listening and responding to others are proclaimed as the sacred manifestations of the reality of the divine love that is the source of each of us. Thus, the sin of adultery is truly a much deeper sin manifesting how we perceive the other and our failure to cherish the other as a child of God.

The second teaching of Jesus centers on the importance of our words as the fundamental method whereby we can bridge the existential chasm that exists between persons. If our words cease to have veracity, in and of themselves, due to the speaker's pattern of articulating falsehoods, only then is it necessary to artificially heighten the situation by invoking additional methods of authentication and trust-worthiness. This necessitates the speaker, whose credibility is in question, to appeal to something else such as oath taking as a method of providing artificial credence to their words. This requires the interjection of something greater to signify that what I am now saying should be believed and accepted by appealing to something of greater authority than my own word as a mechanism of ensuring its credibility. Already, if this is the case, we have accepted a fundamental distortion. For what we are saying is that our word is ordinarily used in a way as to make one question the truth which it expresses. Our pattern of using words without regard to their truth is the foundation of this escalation. It reflects the lost capacity of words to convey meaning, which is at the core of their function, for meaning and veracity are inherently intertwined. Our word is the manifestation of our being and thus, if it is diminished through lying, not only is the individual capacity to share their ideas, thoughts, concerns and knowledge compromised, but the assumed intertwined aspects of communication and truth put in jeopardy on the larger scale of the community. This is not, therefore, merely an individual concern, but potentially the beginning of the essential breakdown of a key thread that makes possible community. Our words are our capacity to bond with each other and corrupting their value through lies fragments the bond between people. It is for this reason that oaths are wrong for they are an attempt to reestablish a fundamental reality that is broken and needs to be addressed directly. The act of appealing to God or any other reality to give weight to one's words when they have lost their inherent trust is useless.

The next law upon which Jesus focuses is the law concerning retribution or "evil for evil" as a method of achieving justice. Here Jesus makes one of His most striking social commentaries. At its core, Jesus is denying the very soundness of retributive justice. He is focusing on the very social fabric which is required of the sustaining of community itself. Responding in kind to any injustice is not capable of sustaining community. In fact, it almost guarantees the escalation of injustice. The Old Testament law of an eye for an eye has no place in the society of people claiming to be God's chosen people. Jesus' focus and passion surrounding this rectification of the method by which any society both maintains order without so weakening the social fabric is the proclamation of a theory of social justice away from retribution and in line with the central belief that only love and forgiveness can truly address issues of a broken covenant between members of a community. Jesus' love and forgiveness is not naïve or out of touch with the less lofty aspects of our humanity. It does not deny that the love, being appealed to, might indeed be a tough love which necessitates certain actions by the community for its self protection, or for the redressing of the wrong committed, it is more focusing on the motivating force that is at the core of the discernment process required to ensure a proper treatment of a brother or sister. As we seek retribution rather than believing that only God can mete out true justice, we give vent to a less noble facet of our natures. Any system of justice under girded from a position of love will see the justice being sought very differently than a system built of retribution and delivering equitable amounts of suffering or injustice.

As a dimension of looking at what should inspire our discernment of meting out justice, Jesus also opines on the inequality associated with the process of the distribution of necessities. Jesus' response to this focuses on the wrongful act of stealing. His unique twist asks the wronged person to honestly assess their real need versus the need of the person who tries to take from you. From Jesus' point of view, if someone takes from you and this does not put you in a position of need, then maybe you ought to give. For the needy have the basic rights required of any person to be fed, clothed, sheltered and cared for. This is then followed quickly by Jesus' discussion of the relationship between members of a community. In Jesus' view we are called to love each other, but not necessarily to like everyone. In this way we are called to do the good for the other regardless of our feelings. These re-interpretations of Judaic Law focus on the centrality of the community, which is comprised of both those we will be fond of and those who may rub us the wrong way. Regardless, we are required to be individuals of self sacrifice, generosity and love.

Jesus is attempting to show how the Jewish leaders of His day who were keepers and teachers of the law had lost touch with its real vitality and were merely engaging in an exercise of regulating external actions. He is also demonstrating His central concern that we appreciate our inter-connectedness as the necessary outcome of our natures. Each of the above re-interpretations of the law focuses on an aspect required to protect the community of believers. Each has the effect of placing God at the center of our being, seeing, hearing, speaking and living. As a result, the dignity and wonder of both individual and community are never lost. It is only in this way that we can escape a life of *non-serviam*.

In another place Jesus again differentiates the Jewish leaders of His day from the truth they were meant to present in their teachings. Once again, Jesus is driving home the chasm between service and the desire to be served, respected and obeyed.

> The scribes and the Pharisees sit on Moses' seat, so practice and observe whatever they tell you—but not what they do. For they preach, but do not practice. They tie up heavy burdens, hard to bear, and lay them on people's shoulders, but they themselves are not willing to move them with their finger. They do all their deeds to be seen by others. For they make their phylacteries broad and their fringes long, and they love the place of honor at feasts and the best seats in the synagogues and

greetings in the marketplaces and being called rabbi by others. But you are not to be called rabbi, for you have one teacher, and you are all brothers. (Matthew 23: 2-8)

This rather direct criticism of the Jewish leaders of His time reflects the contrast between external *pro forma* observance and an interior orientation that gives rise to genuine, authentic practice. The often noted difference between the essentials of the Jewish faith and the practices and teachings of its leaders which Jesus is quick to expose is a trap not singular to the Jewish leaders or this particular time and place. The external focus of these specific individuals in lieu of their internal dispositions is a key manifestation of the subtlety of *non-serviam*. Would that one could look upon these leaders in religion and say that Jesus' complaint was only relevant to the past. In our world we could apply these same observations not merely to many men and women who claim to be religious, but also our civic leaders as well. The source of the observed distortion is once again the ego-centric life. Whenever one's behavior is meant for public consumption, as a method for engendering a certain perception on the part of those in a position to view it, one must be very cautious that behind the public acts there is genuine authentic truth as the motivator. In lieu of this is the potential that the exterior actions are empty and thus imbued with an in-authenticity which points to another motivator. It is in these situations that the distortions of manipulation and is a sure indicator of the realities of manipulation and control at the core of one's moral distortion. Jesus is preoccupied with exposing this central moral flaw and driving those with open hearts and spirits to a way of being that is an authentic manifestation of a mature inner life.

In another text Jesus not only describes once again a symptom of the way of *non-serviam*, but also makes clear the way He is espousing.

> The kings of the Gentiles exercise lordship over them, and those in authority over them are called benefactors, but not so with you. Rather, let the greatest among you become as the youngest, and the leader as one who serves. For who is the greater, one who reclines at table or one who serves? Is it not the one who reclines at table? But I am among you as the one who serves. (Luke 22: 25-28)

Here Jesus speaks most plainly. The orientation of service is core of love and thus required of anyone who is to follow Him. The common acceptance of this world's hierarchy of what is worthy of respect and the place of position and power has no place in Jesus' way.

A life of *non-serviam* is thus a way based on self absorption. It is a way that denies the fluidity of the human person and thus is prone to quick assessments of people and firm judgments. It is also a way of being that denies our fundamental vulnerability and unity as a community. In its place it seeks to control and to manipulate other people and situations and to focus on the self in lieu of the community. It is also a way of being that is comfortable using other people for one's own gain and then dismissing them when they are no longer required. It is a way of life that often attempts to hoard for the admiration of others or as a method of making sure that one can control the unforeseeable future. Most unfortunately, those on this path often limit their capacities to see, to hear and to be generous. It is, as has been said from the very beginning, an orientation based on ego-centricity that is the essence of a life of *non-serviam.*

The essence of the message of Jesus is a way of being that does not forget our creatureliness, but even more embraces its fundamental truths. It is a message centered on self giving and an orientation to others that inherently respects the sanctity of their creations. For Jesus, the individual is not the focus, rather it is the community. Jesus' grasp of the centrality of the community to any authentic life oriented toward the truths of our beings is at the core of almost every message he makes. Our capacity to fool ourselves and to forget what is essential in our lives and for the greater good of the lives around us has been shown as a real temptation throughout human history.

The headlines prominent in today's American papers seem to echo all too clearly the distortions we have presented as core to our moral concerns. We read almost daily about a government deadlocked by self interest. The inherent need for our representatives to be loyal to their constituents and at the same time to be protectors of the nation itself seems a modern impossibility. Our capacity to have the will to address those problems such as our national debt, which have the potential to bring down this wonderful experiment in democracy seem far from either our leaders' minds or their capacity to see the good and do it. Our economy tilts as a result of the unsurpassed greed of many who have forgotten their place as members of a larger concern. Too many have lost their homes, their life savings and their dignity all due to the self absorbed few who only concern themselves with their individual lives. Many donate significant amounts to hospitals, concert halls and numerous other philanthropic concerns, but does this really respond to the issue at hand? Does it somehow mitigate the conscious actions that made many of them recipients of such wealth? Or is it just another attempt to make their ego-centric lives seem more acceptable?

CHAPTER 4

Non-serviam—
Expressed via Power, Arrogance & Selfishness

The way of *non-serviam* offers a multitude of appealing traps on the journey each of us will take in search of the fullness of life. Within the options of the distortion of *non-serviam*, there are a myriad of attributes that can and do appeal to our unique individual natures. The unique proclivity to desire power is one of the most attractive and initially can be one of the most innocuous paths to distortion. From our earliest beginnings as toddlers we begin to learn that power is an operating principle between people. The little boy or girl who aggressively takes away our toy or pushes us around ingrains early in us the reality of power. While most adults will attempt to curtail this in toddlers, it does not remove the reality of one person's ability to deny another what may be theirs. Later, as more mature children, this realization is anything, but wiped away. The playground and most specifically the gym class are often places for power and assertion of oneself over others. Who cannot forget the infamous dodge ball game, or the repeated pattern of the most athletic children being able to pick their teams, often leaving the humiliated and perhaps underdeveloped boy or girl to the end? In these particular instances and in a multiple array of others, children are taught quickly to recognize the strengths and weaknesses of the other and to exploit them and to make the most of them for themselves.

Is it any wonder that power and self assertion for the benefit of the self are traits of our leaders in business and the young men and women choosing to follow them? Again, in and of itself power is not the issue. It is the use of one's personal or physical power in seeking to overtake the other that is being highlighted here. In short, it is one's orientation in viewing one's natural capacities as gifts. Our society is very much oriented toward winning at all costs. Whether this has to do with the college or university you can get into or the choice you make in a profession or even the first position you can land after college. Success at any cost drives our societies' method of promotion and remuneration. Is it any wonder the description of ego-centric lives seems so very familiar to those willing to acknowledge it?

As a culture it is essential that we stand back and reflect on those attributes we reward and encourage. Even though many people will be the first to say that they never have tolerated their children being aggressive and selfish, it is an unfortunate reality that these same people will mix their messages when it comes to sports, academics and university options. While, as an ex-teacher, I will admit many schools have developed aggressive outreach functions to put our young men and women in touch with the less fortunate and suffering, I fear that for many this experience is viewed as an academic requirement to be endured as a resume builder and not truly inculcated into their identities. Our capacity to compartmentalize who we are and what we do can be both a puzzle and a potential concern.

Power has a twin that often is not manifest until one is a bit older. This twin is arrogance. Together power and arrogance are the two most powerful and most destructive roadblocks on the *Way of Service*. Arrogance results when one's natural capabilities enable one to quickly leap ahead of the masses. Arrogance is the result of my internalization of my capabilities and my seeing them as that which separates me from those not as equally capable. It is at this juncture that the realization that one's gifts are indeed unearned gifts and the development of humility must occur or arrogance takes root in their place.

Like a yin and yang arrogance produces in one the desire to acquire things as an expression of its worthiness and power is both the result and often the instigator of this initial orientation toward the world. Both are essential aspects of a *non-serviam* way of being.

It is important to slow down for a more nuanced description of the development of a power oriented stance toward life than we have above, lest we appear to imply that the gift of talent is itself a moral flaw. Having been blest with a good mind or a strong and well coordinated body are not what is being put forth as somehow morally at issue. What is being placed before us is the larger question of how those so blessed view those who may not be blessed in the same way. This aspect of our reflection is also asking us whether we truly understand our gifts as just that, gifts. At the same time, the reality that many of us, blessed with specific talents, also have to work at these. In very few cases are talents fully developed in anyone. They require our participation and our sacrifices. Again the focus here is on how we perceive those who may lack our particular talents and thus may truly need our help or merely our respectful acceptance. Additionally, we must remember that these examples are of normal development and not the developmental challenges of those with extraordinary needs. As infants we experienced the terror of our separateness from all that was originally a unified oneness within our pre-natal state. Once we are born, the world around us seems foreign, filled with terror and the experiences of a vast number of realities, all of which are still merely a horrifying and indistinct other. For the first time we experience the vulnerability of the cold, hunger and often complete and apparently eternal isolation. Even once the infant grasps the reality of the mother, as un-nuanced as that may be the sense of inner terror does not dissipate. Not having a sense of time, the infant cannot place in perspective the absence of the mother and understand that she will return. Each time our mothers are brought back to us, we experience her complete consolation and so begins the initial experience of our grasping wills' desire to hold onto and not let go of that which can and does remove our primal terror.

Our mothers or their substitutes provide us with the fundamental seeds for the belief that suffering can be overcome. Her warm embrace and the food she provides push back the existential terror that the infant experiences in her absence. This is the initiation of the distortion that suffering can be alleviated and that the loneliness of my life can be abrogated by another. Each time she comes and then goes I am forced to increase my awareness that, even in her presence, with the complete satiation she provides, there is the seed of suffering, for I begin to internalize the patterns of coming and going, which stain the perfection of being with her as I begin to realize that her presence cannot and will not be forever.

In these intimate exchanges of love, affection and sustenance, the infant slowly develops a more nuanced ego identity and over time it lets go of the infantile desire to grasp, hold on to and make subject the mother to itself. It is a normal outcome, that the dependence on the mother becomes less narrowly focused. This means that the toddler accepts a larger community of those who are significant to its sense of safety and comfort. As a toddler matures the attachment to its parents can still be very strong and can be expressed in episodes of rage associated with such realities as the parents going out for an evening. These very primal experiences of terror experienced by the evolving development of the self, which while normal in the toddler, if not corrected over time, can be the seeds of distortion which can plague individual development.

As the toddler matures and is introduced to others like themselves the residual distortions of early childhood will be expressed as the child seeks to possess no longer just the mother, but by extension all those things that it identifies as "mine". What parent has not endured the frustration of teaching the child the need for sharing, generosity and the letting go that these situations often imply? This struggle is ongoing and expresses the child's awareness that possessions can express both its capacity to have power over another and at the same time reinforce the child's ego identity. As we have noted, the mother is often one of the earliest objects of the child's grasping. This is often manifest when a new infant is born which requires the mother's attention and concern and the acting out that can often accompany the elder child's desire to control the mother and in a sense to own her. In this case the rage directed at the new infant has sometimes been demonstrated through aggressive acts of cruelty.

What is essential, at this point in our cursory view of human development, is that the young child begins to experience that it is capable of being itself without a dependency on the parents or family. This can only be achieved if the environment of the family encourages a sense of personal safety acceptance and love. It is only through this experience that the child develops a stronger sense of autonomy, which enable it to play, experience new things and extend its circle of intimates. The personal incompleteness experienced by many young children does not simply disappear with age. In fact, the experience of personal inadequacy, can significantly color later human interactions and one's capacity to effectively integrate into new and larger communities. Once the ego is experienced as the energy and source of the child's wants and desires, its initial place at the center of the child is a given as the child continually experiences their central position at the core of all reality. It is thus within the context of normal development that the static ego and its centrality are developed and the opportunity for a correction is possible. In this sense the experience of ego-centricity in a child is not unusual if understood as a developmental period from which the child should be encouraged to emerge. The overindulgent isolating parent could be a significant block to this healthy evolution.

Little of our educative processes directly and consistently address this orientation. In the west what is mostly often addressed are the inappropriate outcomes and actions and thus the symptoms, not the sources. As the child grows and begins its life as a young person, the ego orientation and grasping that characterized the infant have often not been curtailed. This means that at best they have been placed within the social boundaries of acceptable behavior. Certainly, most parents have struggled to enable the child to understand the criticality of sharing and of allowing other children their space without fear of physical violence.

Such things as team sports provide an example of a potential exercise in the re-orientation of the ego-self given correction by the context of the team as a metaphor for the person. The team's ability to be successful requires that each of its individual members be able to accept their place not as the center of the experience, but as one of many. Only through proper cooperation and selfless letting go can the team function. Even here, coaches often experience a talented player who must learn the difficult lesson of not singularizing him or herself, even when doing so might result in more winning games. Only through focusing on each member of the team and generously enabling and aiding others to their optimal participation can the most talented truly ensure the outcome which all the members seek. The dynamics of sports and the struggle between the ego-self and this team orientation is experienced by many young men and women while creating a sense of frustration in many a youth is the proper educating of the young person about the place of both the individual and the community.

The formal educative process prevalent in the west does anything but address and teach this right orientation to life and self. Academic processes place one against the other through the use of curves and rankings through the use of grades, which often segregate individuals into micro-classes and without the proper ego corrections are seldom realized opportunities for aiding others and seeing one's gifts as an opportunity to serve. The individual soon learns the truth that they must compete in order to succeed. This competition distorts both the learning process and the growth of the individual participating in it. This is often compounded by the ongoing distortions already ensconced in the parents, many of whom place inordinate emphasis on achievement rather than learning. The pressure from parents for even pre-high school minds to excel in order to be able to enter the 'right' university is a blatant manifestation of what has become a societal epidemic and most certainly a clear distortion in values.

The young person is not only placed within the context of expanding their minds, expressing their talents and most importantly learning the right way of integrating their weaknesses; they are also simultaneously being encouraged to view this time as their time to demonstrate their superior qualities in opposition to their fellow students. As a result the lessons of the importance of the communal facets of humanity are often barely addressed. One encouraging sign, however, is that some schools now team more talented and advanced students with students who are struggling with this or that subject in peer tutoring programs, both as a way of helping the less-able achieve better academic results and as a method of instilling, in both, a sense of concern and mutual care. We can hope that this sort of practice expands, so that the sense of individualism that later isolates our senses from those in need of our concern and care takes its root at this very formative time is at least somewhat mitigated. This tension between these two very different implicit messages of self development and an appreciation for sharing our gifts with those not so strong in a particular area can often impede the young person's opportunity for complete self appreciation, as well as the full development of their values. Soon the reality that each of us has certain strengths and weaknesses and that it is only through our willingness to share our talents and be open to help to develop our weaknesses can real appreciation of the strength of our communal natures be developed.

The "branding" of education as a kind of marketing distortion now often supersedes what is truly essential. Who one is, who one is becoming and an acute awareness of their essential place in their own and society's future are often completely lost. The idea of being unique now becomes as terrifying as not standing out. If one does not "fit in" or express the social pattern of the group one is often ostracized. Many survive through aggressive separation from the so called "in group" and its values. In this way they soon live in opposition to rather than embracing life in a manner positioned to discover, cherish and develop uniqueness in themselves and others. One way in which this horrific reality has increased in its manifestation is with the young gay or lesbian persons who, as a result of their growing awareness of their sexual feelings, discover that they are not in synchronization with what is described as normative. Significant numbers of these young gay young men and lesbian women have found this state so intolerable that they have chosen their annihilation as preferable to the ongoing choice of discovering how their sexuality can be integrated into their whole beings, and the potential happiness that will be discovered in their ultimately choosing to be who they truly are.

Centers of learning once took it as given that their central task was not merely passing on academic knowledge, but the more essential role of forming the whole man or woman through a focus on the truth of life, one's responsibilities and how one fits within the social fabric of school, community, nation and, ultimately, the larger world. The artificial measuring, ranking and comparing that increasingly dominate schools can be mistaken for ontological classifications of personal worth. This is, of course, a monumental distortion. The underlying belief that the successful student or athlete or, in time, executive is somehow inherently superior to oneself is a real danger that must be addressed.

The creation of the essential human attributes of empathy and compassion require that one reflect on the process of the creation of the various concentric circles of intimacy and concern associated with childhood and continuing through one's maturation. Each of these layers, beginning with the immediate family, then the extended family, one's immediate neighborhood, one's school and so on are essential expressions of development and maturity. The opposite reality which slowly collapses these concentric circles of concern, identity and emotional connection is equally essential. It is only through the experience of the interdependence of oneself with others and the continued introduction of the growing person to others who may be different from oneself that this process can happen.

Both empathy and compassion require that each individual be able to understand himself in his essential relatedness to others who may not at first seem to be similar. It requires the educative process that exposes and destroys the artificial distinctions that we often embrace to justify our unconscious belief that "the other" is not worthy of empathy or compassion because they are essentially different. Education is critical in the process through which these rings of indifference and abstraction are challenged and slowly collapsed such that the ego-self can appreciate its essential interconnectedness with all of life. As a result the critical interdependence of human existence can be appreciated as expressive of our intimacy and interdependence. The previous lack of acceptance, resulting from layers of abstract assumptions which radiated from the distorted static ego can be overcome. Learning empathy and compassion facilitates the collapse of these layers of alienation and with them mistaken impressions of degrees of importance implied by their proximity to the ego-self.

Ironically perhaps, the distortions born in our earliest experiences and never directly addressed may now be displayed in adulthood in ways that appear socially appropriate and which often bring the rewards we seek. As one enters one's profession one will focus one's efforts and attentions on developing those skills that will best ensure the success and progress which our ego-selves require to sustain our sense of worth. Often, these successes do come and with them our capacity to earn more and to grow in the esteem of others. During this period we learn not just the necessary technical facets of our positions, but also the social rules, values and actions which are seen as required for our continued advancement. Each time we are recognized and advanced both our professional expertise and our ability to manifest the social and cultural values of the organization are reinforced not only in us, but in those who see us advancing and are desirous of advancement for themselves. It is important to be cognizant of the fact that the externality of the individual's sense of worth continues to be the focus.

With advancement comes the requirement to enter into the new role of managing and directing others. With this, a new experience of power is introduced. We now have the ability directly to control the actions of others. If not rightly understood and integrated into a properly developed set of values this new responsibility may be seen as the ability to use others to best guarantee our continued personal success. Not only are we now aware of this power, but also more cognizant of the ongoing levels of power that lay before one as rungs on a ladder. If still ensconced in our ego distortion, we will fail to grasp with equal attention that the position of management is a commitment to cherish and expand the talents placed at one's disposal. Without this critical appreciation, those placed in our care will at best be seen as the extension of ourselves and essential to our own success.

Of course those around us such as our parents, friends and family continue to express their increased pride in our success. We ourselves also begin to feel the sense of pride associated with the levels of progression and the economic privileges that promotion now makes available to us and our families. The reality is that this experience of success and the power it brings is seldom appreciated for very long as we soon live within the new bounds of our increased pay and the symbolism of an office. Thus the experience of power and the adulation that comes with it are addictive in the truest sense. We require continued recognition and promotion, and may find ourselves more aggressively pursuing them and increasingly impatient for this success.

In distortion, these successes and the increased responsibility that they make real are now seen as the vehicles for our progression. The people we manage are rewarded in direct relation to their abilities to contribute to our ongoing success. Those under our care who manifest a singular set of talents which bring them notice might become occasions of concern, lest their light shine too brightly. In response to this a manager may seek to besmirch their reputations by making negative observations to those who might have noticed their potential.

Self pride, as the more acceptable side of arrogance, is a real, important and often positive outcome of success. Few appreciate it as the source of the drive for increased power as well. Pride becomes pernicious when it is twisted such that it is a significant driver for un-restrained advancement, acquisition and economic power. Arrogance as both the instigator of action and the outcome of action, if not rightly integrated into the self, is a powerful distortion of one's self understanding, of one's relationships.

Orientations of arrogance and power make the opportunity to serve almost impossible. For in achieving professional success, we begin to believe that we are truly deserving and thus special. Even when the promotion is within a context of service itself, such as in religious life, it can manifest itself as anything but the call to greater humility and generosity. As a result, the individual whose life orientation is meant to be one of humility and striving for authentic self actualization often discovers that the manner by which they embrace their positions reveals an orientation of lording their power over their brothers and sisters in community. This distortion can also manifest itself through persons who become self absorbed in their positions and soon define themselves by their roles. The superior who must be in control of everything and who soon becomes the center of all within the community either through the exalted sense that they alone can do what needs to be done correctly or their inability to truly embrace their role as the one responsible for the effective tending of the garden that is their community soon reveals a posture of distance from those for whom they are responsible. This can often be revealed by an inability to be present to those they lead, to truly listen and hear them. It is almost always demonstrated by a lack of empathy and compassion for those for whom they should be most concerned. St. Benedict referred to the good abbot as a physician who knows his patients and is sensitive to the approach taken in their continued care so as not to place too much burden on those not able to bear it or not enough for those who need the challenge.

Indeed the crisis of vocations that haunts the west is in great part the result of the fact that many of the communities and congregations which should be attracting young men and women are in fact often perceived as not significantly different from the secular corporations of the world. In religious life, the higher one is lifted the more intense is their call to love, to cherish and to shape those under their care. The capacity to be attuned to their charges and to be sensitive and generous with their attention and concern are critical aspects of the head of a religious community in which the leader is to be seen as Christ. Without this appreciation by each of the superiors that their first and most sacred duty is in the ongoing concern and care for the souls with which they have been entrusted the religious house cannot manifest the love, acceptance, generosity and humility that are required for a true school of the Lord's service.

The lack of right orientation in the superior can lead to the placing of responsibility on other religious who are themselves not in the position to accept this responsibility as a call to serve their fellow religious community members. The result is truly destructive of the future of the religious order. It would not be an overstatement to say that religious life is a life of service first to the community and second to the larger society. For if one cannot rightly serve one's brothers or sisters how can one truly serve God's people? In this situation what often appears as service is the courting of those members of society that can feed the ego-centric self. In this way the religious or priest may actually be giving scandal to a population not insensitive to the honed attention focused on particular sheep within the flock.

It should be expected that religious communities are comprised of men and women whose entire orientation is to bring wholeness, healing and salvation to each other through an infinity of acts of mutual service, humility, generosity and love. If this were but true, religious houses would be unable to meet the demands of a culture which has discovered the ultimate emptiness of power and possessions. Our world cries out for such places and such people. It cries out not for the perfect, but for the broken who are courageous enough to offer their imperfect and incomplete selves to each other for mutual correction and the palliative which only true self awareness, compassion and love can bring.

The true perspective of the meaning of my life, how I am called to promote, heal and teach others so that they may achieve personal actualization, peace and the honing of their talents for the benefit of all is essential for the healing needed at all levels of our world. It is only through our acceptance of our distortions and our equal determination and courage in addressing them that the appreciation of each person we come into contact with as a unique being essential to the evolution of our world will engender genuine concern, care and healing love. It is the undeniable reality of our interconnectedness and interdependence which is the foundation of our distortions of power and arrogance are choking life from us all. Behind the distortions of arrogance and power is the infantile desire to control. It is a rejection of our lives as processes and journeys and in tandem the rejection of others as occasions of unfolding and potential flourishing.

These distortions have been described as they often present themselves in corporations, professions and even in religious institutions. They are distortions born in infancy and which must be addressed and transformed in and through the educative process that exists in our homes, our academic institutions and as part of the process of religious formation. Without this transformation, one cannot be surprised by the infantile behavior that is so apparent even at the very top of our commercial, governmental and religious institutions.

As a result our society stands in crisis. The economic conditions of our vastly rich land teeter on ruin. The robber barons of the late nineteenth century seem to have returned to regain control of most of the economic power. The middle class continues to erode as the possessors of money and power play the system to sustain what they have acquired with little genuine concern for those increasing numbers who must go without and who become increasingly marginalized. Philanthropy within this construct appears often to become merely a method of quieting what might remain as the still small voice of truth within many of these titans. In reaction many young men and women band together convinced that no other avenue exists for them. These gangs do not seek to bring right to the distortion so pervasive in our society, but seek an alternative route to achieve what those at society's top have seemingly declared as rightfully theirs and theirs alone. Their methods might be different and they may prey on the weak and the ill through, for instance, the selling of narcotics, but can one really say that our corporate leaders and in some cases our political leaders have not engaged in the same activity through more socially acceptable means?

Non-serviam is essentially the distortion of "me first." It is the ego-centric desire to win. This winning is the attempt to propel myself to the top or as close as I can get. It is the belief that what is essential are my needs, my wants and my desires with only enough sharing to enable me to feel secure and in control. It is in a real sense the model we proposed of the chess set in which the king is the only real piece. Every other piece is there to ensure that the king does not lose what has been acquired, taken and horded. Arrogance and power are the essential motivators and methods for the achieving of this end.

PART 2

Serviam—A Life Choice

CHAPTER 5

Introduction—*Serviam*

This second half of our reflection is based on the life and teachings of Jesus, as reflected upon in the Gospels, with specific sensitivity to the early Christian community's appreciation of how Jesus appreciated evil as part of the human struggle toward redemption. Whereas the first half of this reflection has focused on the many opportunities in our lives for going astray, this portion of our reflection will focus on the constructive elements of the moral framework created by Jesus and His early followers. Many readers of the New Testament may be surprised by how few moral proclamations of Jesus there are. This should not lead one to the conclusion that appreciating the moral dynamics of human life was anything but essential to Jesus.

Jesus saw the moral capacity of the human person as an essential element of the divine spark which animates each one of us. The moral dimension of humanity consists of more than the individual choices made over the course of our personal lives. The moral tension which imbues life itself is only resolved through the communal nature of humanity. The realities of non-moral evil and the kind of evil resulting from human choice can only be resolved through the communal opportunities of service, generosity and love; the outcome of evil is suffering, which can lead to hopelessness, isolation and an anxiety. Only through our acceptance of our communal natures and their corresponding responsibilities which call us to serve can hope replace despair in all its manifestations.

The reality of good and evil, or the moral framework is the back-drop of human life on earth. Going forward, I have chosen to avoid the concepts of "good" and "evil". The reason is that both these very good English words have become encrusted with a lot of connotations and not a few theological weights. It is therefore easier to avoid the words then to try to qualify them to bound their meanings. The moral dimensions of human existence are played out in the dynamic tension between the beneficial and the malignant happenings that are part of the very fabric of our existences. This understanding is far richer in meaning than the concept that there is an additive element to existence resulting from an external demonic force. Life's moral drama which envelops all life and very specific aspects of human existence is a combination of our personal, individual capabilities and the concrete results of the exercising of our wills. Each individual, generation and period of human unfolding reveals the inherent tension between beneficial and malignant reality in the human drama. Jesus not only entered this drama as God-made-man, but as one called to shape the nature of this external and internal struggle. Despite the beliefs of many of the early Christians, Jesus did not come to put an end to this essential tension. He did, however, come to make clear nuances of this dynamism that had yet to be fully understood.

The tension between beneficial and malignant reality (both resulting from human choices and non-moral natural occurrences) did not disappear as a result of the incarnation. The human processes of giving birth to itself as a species and of the unfolding world in which we live cannot be brought to completion without both fundamental realities identified by us as beneficial and malignant. These realities understood as both internal and external realities are the dynamics essential to our potential redemption and salvation. If anything, Jesus' life, as a lived event, as well as his preaching gave greater meaning to these dimensions of human existence. It was as if Jesus highlighted these antithetical dimensions to highlight them and by so doing the struggle would be made heightened. Beneficial and malignant realities were now to envelop the entire process begun in creation and in constant movement toward its culmination. To the surprise of many, both then and now, the struggle between these two necessary aspects of life are essential elements in our reaching fulfillment, our salvation. In opposition to the rather simplistic medieval notions of the opposition of separate powers of ultimate good and ultimate evil, Jesus presents our challenge as the discovery of the right balance of both of these dimensions of human existence, which are mutually required aspects of life and redemption.

Eradicating malignancy was not Jesus' mission. For malignancy is as essential to the world and our beings as is our capacity for goodness. Jesus places before us these mutually constitutive dimensions - beneficence and malignancy as the very tension of existence, which requires not merely individual acts of goodness, but, as critically, communal participation in the healing and enduring of suffering and anguish—the noblest good of which humanity is capable. It is only within this context of malignancy, suffering, and anguish, as the process of giving birth to salvation, which we can hope to discover redemption.

This portion of our reflection focuses on service as the most robust method of expressing a way of living such a redemptive life.

Any introduction to *A Life of Service* would be remiss if it did not begin by reflecting upon the supreme act of service that was exemplified in God becoming human. This mystery, before which we can only stand in awe, manifests the many attributes of service such as humility, lowliness, generosity and most specifically the supreme act of love.

Essential to understanding service is the realization that it can be expressed in two different ways. As expressed in a passive mode, service is most simply the offering of one's self for the use of another. While this distinction may initially seem very subtle it is essential. Passive service results when one is confronted by the need of another. For example, an elderly woman might request my seat on a train or bus. While I might respond very graciously and thus serve her, the act is in this sense passive. Without her request, I might not have even noticed her due to the fact that I was reading a newspaper or merely zoned out after a long day.

The second mode of service is the active mode. It is this kind of service that is paramount. No one would deny the service offered by the gentleman described above, but it is not service to its fullest. Active service is first my willed openness to the world outside of me. In this sense, service is an active choice of an individual to be attuned to their world. It is the result of the individual's free choice to remove the ego as the core of their life orientation, which creates the space for one to be attuned to another.

As a result this active posture we are in a position to perceive a need and then to make the ensuing choice of self offering to aid in addressing this need. Using the example of the elderly woman and the gentleman on the train, the scenario might unfold as follows. The gentleman gets on the train and finds a seat. As he prepares to read his paper he notices that the car is filling up very fast and that seats are also filling up. He also notices an elderly women coming in the subway car and it is apparent that she will not get one of the few seats left. The gentleman then asks the elderly women if she would like to take his seat.

Our focus going forward will be on active service. For it is active service that is the proper orientation of both one's self and one's free will. Active service and sacrifice are tightly coupled realities. It is as the result of our active service that we are open to making a sacrifice of ourselves. This kind of sacrifice requires an openness of one's life to the potential needs of another. In this sense active service is a pre-condition to sacrifice. Sacrifice is thus not always bloody as in martyrdom. Sacrifice is the offering of oneself to another for their use. The resulting good can range from the ultimate self offering to the smallest of gifts such as that of one's time. This relationship between service and sacrifice is made clear in our vernacular ways of considering the duty of entering the military in a time of war. We use the phrase "entering the service" and the potential that this service may entail is the sacrifice of oneself for one's country. As we continue, the distinction between active and passive service will no longer be stressed. Whenever we speak of service we shall be speaking of active service.

It is important that we grasp the relationship between service and sacrifice in our human condition. Only then can we hope to grasp the wonder and dignity of both, when considering the act of God becoming man. The key aspects of service made manifest by the act of God in the incarnation reveal not only the essential characteristics of the divinity, but even more an increased revelation of the nature of our humanity, created *ad imago Dei*. A brief focus on the nature of God and how it has evolved over the centuries will provide both a deeper appreciation of the role of God in our understanding of service and as a central paradigm of authentic human living.

At the core of the classical notion of God has been the Platonic concept of absolute "Being". This reality of being, promulgated by Plato, was the perfect form or idea that encompassed all other realities and yet was more than the mere additive grouping of these. For Plato, absolute being was the same as absolute Truth, Beauty, and Goodness. In Platonic thought these very special facets of absolute being were themselves absolute and not particular. Thus, where we might experience something as beautiful in our material world, it would be considered an imperfect shadow of the fullness of Beauty itself. It is, important to note however, that for a Platonist any specific thing in the material world that is beautiful is so because it participates in the very nature of absolute Beauty. While very poetic, this concept of participation was to render a platonic cosmology as more applicable to a kind of mysticism than a rigorous method of understanding reality. It is important, however, to accept that every philosopher of merit, and truly Plato is one, grasps at least one facet of reality in a manner that unveils a truth many others will forget. Plato understood that there was something at the heart of life that was beyond our capacity to measure, describe or contain in our small finite minds and this was the reality of life, i.e. Being itself.

The early church theologians used the Platonic concept of absolute Being as a method of articulating the reality of God.

As a result, absolute Being was described as unchanging (immutable), all powerful (omnipotent) and unlimited in any way. Initially, the Christian notion of God would take on these very descriptors. Over time, however, this purely Platonic notion of God began to raise as many issues as it initially resolved. For, if God were merely the philosophical concept of absolute Being now wrapped in theological garb, His nature as immutable would make such pivotal realities as God becoming man in time at best beyond reason.

While certainly there are many aspects of God that are not open to human understanding and thus remain mysteries, the idea of God as contradictory to the reason he imbedded within us is usually a signal of our deficiency in understanding and not an acceptance of a mystery of God as being irrational; for our reason is, if you will, a slice of the divine reason that both informs and sustains all that is.

As a result of the unchanging nature of the divinity, the Incarnation was appreciated as a complete mystery for many theologians and philosophers as it appeared to contradict the classical Greek understanding of God's immutability. This conundrum has as its source the initial literal lifting of our understanding of God from the Greek Platonists and the later Neo-Platonists. Only in time did the church come to appreciate that the God exposed through the life and teaching of Jesus of Nazareth was quite different from both the Greek classical notions of being and the God of the Old Testament.

As the community of the Church continued to reflect on the mystery of the Christ event and its implications for how it conceived of God, it began to grasp dimensions of the Father that included the integration of Jesus' revelations. The central message that ran through all of Jesus' teachings and the call crucial to each human being's life, as well as how Jesus experienced His Father was always through the centrality of love.

A natural outcome that resulted from the centrality of love preached by Jesus was its direct enrichment of the believing community's understanding of the God. Abba, the intimate moniker used by Jesus when He spoke of and to God, was a key to how the community of believers would come to an evolution of their understanding of God. This realization initiated a change from perceiving God as the supreme being of the Greeks to seeing the Father as the limitless and all powerful source and end of love. It was now possible to appreciate our God in a radically different light. Gone would be the idea of God as the Greeks initially conceived, and now would emerge the revelation of the Father as the supreme reality of love. What it appears that the Greeks never grasped was that God's perfection was in the mystery of God's self expression. Only in coming to understand Jesus and His message could this reality come to the fore.

This concept of love is not the touchy-feely idea that is promulgated in teen-age love songs or Hollywood movies. This reality of love is the eternal act of generativity and self expression which love is and which are the core of both God and all that emanates from, and is created by, this Love. It is from this perspective that we can only truly come to understand our humanity. As created from this single source of love we are only truly alive when we become its instruments. It is thus within this context of love that we discover ourselves and our purpose.

It is as part of the gift of Jesus' life and sharing that this nuance of the essence of our Creator was passed on from the Son to us. It is also through the vehicle of the Son as the perfect expression of the love of the Father that we come to see our call and our burden.

> Beloved, let us love one another, because love is from God; everyone who loves is born of God and knows God. (1 John 4:7)

Thus rather than merely accepting the Platonic notion of immutability as a necessary element of pure being postulated by the Greeks, the Christian faith came to understand and accept the full ramification of Jesus concerning His Father. God's immutability was not questioned, but was now comprehended as the immutable expression of His nature as love itself. This truth manifests itself first in the act of creation and then in the ongoing sustaining of all that was created. It continued in the ongoing wooing of the Chosen People of the Old Testament and it has begun its culmination in the act of God becoming man. It is in this penultimate reality of the Incarnation that Jesus was to bring to us a more complete and intimate understanding of His Father as Love and through this a more perfect understanding of ourselves and our role in the returning of all things in time to the love of the Father.

It is from this perspective that service as the proper orientation of our human lives must be understood and freely chosen. In this manner, the ultimate service embraced by the Father in sending His Son is both the model and the call for proper human existence. To understand this framework one must remember the undeniable, of embracing all humanity in the free gift of the Son. What religions often separate, Christ calls together. While religious institutions reveal the brokenness of their humanity, Christ's message and life stand uncorrupted and incorruptible. This in no way intends to suggest that religious expression of our beliefs and faiths are unnecessary, rather to force our focused insight on the fact that they are human institutions and as such imperfect expressions of humanity's desire to be true to the one who gave us life.

For the service which Jesus embraced was to free humanity from the shackles of sin and death as well as to communicate a greater understanding of the Father.

So we have known and believe the love that God has for us. God is love, and those who abide in love abide in God, and God abides in them. (1 John 4:16)

In a similar way, the church now embraced God's omnipotence as not merely His power to do anything, but as His unlimited capacity to express the love He is. Thus the Father's offering of the Son to be born as man and to be wrapped in our human condition was an ongoing expression of His immutability and omnipotence. In the Incarnation neither God's supreme power nor His unchanging nature was in any way compromised; they both expressed coherently the love that is their source.

This shift from the philosopher's concept of being as most descriptive of God involved the deeper and more meaningful acceptance of the God of Abraham and Isaac and Christ as the perfect unlimited and supreme reality of love. The result was the church's ongoing reflection on God and his Son, sent to free humanity from sin, error and death, and an even greater understanding of God as a communal unity comprised of the

Father, the Son and the Holy Spirit, as expressive of the binding together of the Father and Son in the eternal perfection of love, which she is (classically the Holy Spirit was the feminine facet of God).

This desire to understand the incarnation as a consistent reality within the very nature of God is in no way an attempt to diminish the mystery of mysteries of the unprecedented self-offering of God to humanity in the person of Jesus. To truly appreciate the Incarnation one must grasp it as the act of incomparable selflessness, generosity and love. It is the perfect act of service and sacrifice. For only by taking on our humanity could God truly redeem His broken creation. Only through the supreme love of the Creator becoming the creature could salvation be offered to his creature, both steeped in sin and subject to death.

In this manner the Incarnation expresses the supreme act of service and sacrifice of our God who chose to take on the lowliness of His creature as the perfect opportunity to expose Himself and to communicate more fully His nature. It was as a result of the Christ event that humanity was to come both to understand the depth of divine love and to make specific the way and the choice of salvation. For by letting us know Him more fully through the Son, and through our capacity to meditate on the Son's life and the message not only do we come to know the Father better, but we come to know ourselves who are the potential images of God.

I ask not only on behalf of these, but also on behalf of those who will believe in me through their word, that they may all be one. As you, Father, are in me and I am in you, may they also be in us, so that the world may believe that you have sent me. The glory that you have given me I have given them, so that they may be one, as we are one, I in them and you in me, that they may become completely one, so that the world may know that you have sent me and have loved them even as you have loved me. (John 17: 20-23)

Thus began the development of our appreciation of the one true god as being a *communio* or communion of persons, which we have articulated as the mystery of the Trinity. For only in the reality of the Trinity, which was to express the essential communal nature of our monotheistic God could we truly come to understand the fullness of our own natures as also inherently *communio*.

The church discovered in the unity of God, the relational nature of the Father, the creator, the Son, the perfect expression of the Father; and the Holy Spirit, the love that emanates from and between Father and Son and which overflows in its abundance as expressed in all creation. While it is not our intent to develop a pedagogical development of the Trinity, this essential nature of God as a *communio* or communion is important in two ways, as revealing something new about God, and as revealing a fundamental truth about us, which will certainly color our reflection on service.

Appreciating the communal relationship internal to the one true God has far reaching ramifications for us. Over the course of human history the question as to the nature of humanity as either highly individualistic or as inherently communal has been batted about among thinkers concerned for what we would be like in the artificial contrivance of a state of nature. This 'state of nature' was the intellectual artifice of humanity outside of what many philosophers once thought to be the corrupting influence of society or culture. Some thinkers proposed that humanity's temperament was revelatory of a radical individualism which has given birth to societies as the mechanism for individuals to achieve their singular wants and desires. It is individualism which required our social constructs as the only way of keeping our selfish drives in appropriate check. For the creation of society became the necessary method for ensuring each of us our optimal capacity for achieving and maintaining our desires. Society was thus postulated as the necessary construct for protecting ourselves from ourselves. It is this underlying acceptance that each of us is selfish, brutish and so self preoccupied as to make us dangerous to each other without the proper constraints of society which lie at the heart of many pre and post Enlightenment thinkers.

Many events in human history seem to make this characterization not only plausible, but frightfully expressive of a basic reality. It appears however, spurious to take examples of humanity at their worst as the basis for defining our natures. No one who has the slightest notion of history can deny what our worst aspects are capable of, but surely this is only part of the story.

As Christians, we cannot accept this slanted view or interpretation of humanity. It is both counter to the dignity of our creation and our beings formed to be the potential images of God. In coming to understand God as inherently communal, the church has also come to more fully accept the fact that each human individual, though always sacred and always an end in themselves, is only provided the optimal context for unfolding in *communio*. In this sense, the community is primary, both in importance and ordinally for it is the necessary milieu in and through which the human person can be formed. Lest one conclude from this that this communal aspect of our natures is required merely for our basic formation, it must be stated that it is also the necessary requirement for our achieving our fullness as individuals and ultimately for the redemption of our species.

Without this safe and supportive context in which the gifts and values of the human person are provided the proper soil from which to sprout and grow, can anything but the monsters alluded to above, which pepper our history, be brought forth? Where the individualists have made their error is in using distorted human beings as the focus for their construct of humans in a state of nature. If one begins with the outcome of a human person given life within a healthy, stable and value rich climate imbued with love, the outcome would be quite different and thus the need for the community is understood as the precursor to the unfolding of what is really a human being and not a, sad, broken, scarred and maladjusted individual. It is, in fact, this very context which is required as a precursor to the capacity of the individual to set aside their ego ensconced at their core in infancy and early childhood. Without this significant step in our maturation the individual will grow within a context of fear, and remain the grasping, manipulative and self preoccupied child, only now with the full powers of an adult.

Evelyn Waugh's famous novel *Brideshead Revisited* pivots around this very issue of the essential role of the family in the creation of human beings capable of achieving their potential and discovering peace in their lives. Waugh presents the Marchmain family, a noble aristocratic family, steeped in the Roman Catholic faith of their mother. It is her internalization of this faith which, rather than making the mother whole and imbued with the love of her God, has made her as rigid and inflexible as the marble statues that pepper the estate. She has no tolerance or capacity to love the sinner as Jesus did. She demands perfection, foreign to the human condition. In this way rather than bringing life to those she loves, she suffocates them in expectation and her ongoing disappointment.

After a stint in WWI, her husband, Lord Marchmain flees from Lady Marchmain to Venice where he immediately takes a mistress, Cara. In a poignant scene, Cara is alone with Charles Ryder, an intimate friend of Sebastian, one of the sons of Lord and Lady Marchmain. Cara takes this opportunity to reveal the essence of the Marchmains to Charles;

> Do you think he [Lord Marchmain] loves me?...He does not. Then why does he stay with me? I will tell you; because I protect him from Lady Marchmain. He hates her...My friend is a volcano of hate. He cannot breathe the same air as she. He will not set foot in England because it is her home...Sebastian hates her too...they are full of hate. (Evelyn Waugh, *Brideshead Revisited*, Back Bay Books, NY, 1999, pp. 102-103)

This hatred is the response of the husband and children to the unyielding requirement of Lady Marchmain for them to be perfect. It is not a hatred that lies easily at the surface of their consciousness, but rests like banked down embers eating away at them. Ultimately, it drives Sebastian to the remoteness of Morocco and alcoholism. It twists and mars the external beauty of her daughter Julia and creates in the eldest son, Brideshead, and the youngest daughter Cordelia, an unflinching need to live in desperate search of her approval even, well past her death.

This short exposition of Waugh merely typifies the centrality of the family and the necessity of this as a loving and supportive community. The intimate family (regardless of its varied permutations in modern society) is the very first and most critical manifestation of the communion required to give the proper environment for the growth of a healthy human person. This is not merely a street address, or house in which a child is brought forth, but the loving and nurturing context in which the full participation of those who have accepted the responsibility to nurture this unique being is consistently present. It is only in and through this initial community that the emerging individual can discover the larger society and world not as something to be feared and controlled, but the larger environment in which one can discover and develop one's strength and identity.

The stresses on this initial and most intimate core of family are many. There are too many situations in which either the family has been broken or in our modern times, where it is laid waste to the economic stresses pulling at its very fabric as modern life now often requires multiple members of this family unit to work in order to keep the family two steps ahead of the creditors. It is not possible to get around the truth that the family must be present as the necessary formative contexts of those lives being developed within it. Unfortunately, institutional stand-ins for parents do not seem to be working. In those cases where the extended family can offer to provide support, it can often be the best alternative.

Before we allow the reality of the nuclear family to fade, we should look hard at what we value so highly as a culture that it is worth our choosing to let dissolve the first intimate community into which new lives emerge. Without the nuclear family we are lost. For as the corner stone of human existence, the communication of our values, our culture and the learning's of one generation can only be passed on to those yet too young to comprehend, but never too young to be shaped.

As a society we must face the effects of the already lost generations. We must look hard at our values and our commitments to the young men and women who are our future and our making. Letting our children evolve based on the loose federation of other children cannot and will not create an environment in which what is most noble in us can be discovered and brought forth.

Already too many of our children do not have enough time to be children. Sadly, many have been allowed to detach themselves from the intimate context of love and nurturing that must be the nuclear family. Sometimes this is the outcome of unhealthy families and at other times it is the result of the fact that no real family was there to begin with. One always hears the cry to take back our streets and our cities. If this is truly what we desire we had better take back our families first.

Service, as that to which we are called, is first what one generation owes the next in ensuring that all opportunities are made to ensure the health and whole emergence of the generation to follow. While we have initially focused on the family as the most intimate context for shaping the next generation, it would be incomplete if we did not recognize the larger community's shared part in ensuring the health of our next generation. I do not believe that we have embraced this aspect of service that we owe to each other and especially to our young. In many respects it is this larger community that should be the reality of inter-connected concern and love that makes up for the limits within any family.

Hopefully, the discussion of the human dynamics of the divine communal reality has struck a note of resonance in us. For if our theological reflections do not touch our lives as expressing the deepest truths of our world and our beings then they are indeed empty. Without these sacred realities from where can one discover who one is, what if anything is our purpose in living and what are the values that we should cling to as protecting us from the endless darkness that can so easily abide deep in our souls? Without these truths wrapped in myths and mystery, which continue to call forth from us something more, which is certainly there, and necessitates nurturing to be brought forth, is life worth living? At the same time, we must be leery of the rigorist tendency given poignant example in the sad life of Lady Marchmain, which can stand in for love and thus distort the essential core that we are called to embrace and to extend to each other.

The pinnacle of the theology of *communio* as descriptive of the mystery of our God is most profoundly expressed in the letter of St. Paul to the Philippians. For it is here that God, the Father, and God, the Son, in their eternal coexistence and love are described as emptying themselves of their perfect union so that the perfection of their love might be more fully expounded by the Word, which is the Son offered to humanity in time for the opportunity to know the Father more intimately and as the result the fullness of the communio of the trinity. For it is only through our discovery of God's internal nature as love expressed as both divine completeness and the superabundance of existence "that we truly grasp the centrality of humility as a key fact of love.

As a result of this perfect expression of love as the very nature of God, the path of salvation is now made clear as is the choice offered to all of us. St. Paul's language expresses unequivocally that the very act of God taking on humanity's lowliness by being wrapped in the limitations and vulnerability of the human condition is not contrary to the attributes of immutability and omnipotence, but rather the perfect articulation of the nature of the divine which is love.

> Let the same mind be in you that was in Christ Jesus, who, though he was in the form of God, did not regard equality with God as something to be exploited, but emptied himself, taking the form of a slave, being born in human likeness. And being found in human form, he humbled himself and became obedient to the point of death—even death on a cross. (Philippians 2: 5-9)

St. Paul articulates the epicenter of the Incarnation by highlighting Jesus of Nazareth's not grasping at His equality with God, but instead His free emptying of himself and taking on the form of man, or more specifically a slave. The depth of meaning which undergirds this wonderful passage as well as the hymn, "*Christus factus est.*", begins with the coupling of this act of supreme love with the co-eternal nature of the Son as expressed in the theologically rich opening of the Gospel of St. John.

> In the beginning was the Word, and the Word was with God, and the Word was God. He was with God in the beginning.
> Through him all things were made; without him nothing was made that has been made. In him was life,

and that life was the light of men. The light shines in the darkness, but the darkness has not understood it. (John 1: 1-5)

It is through this light that we seek the mysteries and myths of our faith. It is also this light for which we search ceaselessly as we gaze into each other's eyes. It is the clarity of this light which provides our capacity to see and then our free capacity to choose to turn our faces toward it in hope and love.

Darkness is real and it can permeate our very beings to the detriment of ourselves and each other. Discovering the light and letting it both illuminate our ways and our souls is our fundamental choice. It will not illumine us assertively, but requires our invitation and our making a proper home for it. It is a light which illumines all in love. It is not nor should it ever be considered a light for illuminating the imperfections of others. Jesus, who is this light, embraced each person as they were. Once embraced in love, then one could unfold in full realization that they were loved fully and completely as they are.

Together these two passages from St. Paul and St. John, articulate the centrality of love as the Divine force that is the source of God's self offering in the gift of his Son to the entire world in the incarnation. The multiple extraordinary elements of the mystery of the life that was Jesus of Nazareth present themselves in a manner which has led to ongoing theological discussion and reflection. For the life of the Son made man is the unparalleled disclosure of the countless nuances of this *koinonia*, or pouring out of Jesus' splendor each as awesome in nature as to lead theologians to wonder as to which should be recognized as supreme.

The three primary events that stand above all the others within the life of Jesus of Nazareth are the Incarnation, the Crucifixion, and the Resurrection. These three distinct moments are imbued with such perfect expressions of love; meaning, self revelation and service that discerning which should stand as the primary has been an open debate for centuries. Is the Incarnation alone the supreme act of wonder? Or is it the immolation and death which stands as the pinnacle of self offering which should be the unequivocal point of our devotion? Finally, could both these options be merely prerequisites to the Resurrection as the true apex of the Christ event?

This question presents for our consideration the Incarnation no longer considered in isolation from Jesus' ultimate death. For as a human, Jesus' birth entailed and required His death as two inextricably intertwined realities. The free choice of Jesus who accepted the kind of death He was to suffer as the continued self offering, began in the Son who deigned to become man and in the fullness of His time consummated this self offering through His willed acceptance to freely make the journey to Jerusalem.

It is not being suggested that Jesus had pre-knowledge of a supernatural kind as to the specifics of His death. The kind of death of death he was to undergo only became increasingly clearer over time. As a result of Jesus' choices to confront the religious authorities of His day and to continue His journey to Jerusalem it would become ever more clear that his death would most probably not be from old age. Rather that He knew from the very start of His mission and the acceptance of His call and His unwavering dedication to serve and the unfolding reality that He was on a collision course with the authorities. As these moments of conflict increased and the inherent tension between the Jewish leaders of the time, and His free determination to speak the truth, which pitted Him against them and all they stood for, the inevitability of His destruction became ever clearer. The crucifixion was not a necessary requirement, but His death as the result of His human birth, as man, was.

From this perspective, the birth of Jesus and His death, both understood as free gifts must be revered in their singularity. Both can and should be celebrated as the church does, but to search for either to somehow be the more perfect expression would be a failure to grasp their fundamental unity as one consistent and ongoing choice to do the Father's will. Thus while each is worthy of our worship and meditation in their own right, it is only in their unity as Jesus' singular commitment to His Father that their full meaning and wonder can be disclosed.

The Resurrection as the final act of this sacred drama is unique, for it is the Father's act of love now bestowed on the Son in recognition of Jesus' free and unwavering alignment of His will to that of His Father as it became clear to Him. It is the Father's radical gift to the Son in return for His having made himself available to humanity in the Incarnation and in His death. It is the perfect expression of love which brought back the Son to the Father and opened heaven to all those who would embrace the way of Jesus. The Resurrection is the fulfillment of God's actions and commitment to the Son and humanity. Jesus conquers death through love and promises us that, if we love as he loved. We too will overcome death's final word. For as St. Paul most wonderfully expressed,

O death, where is your victory? O death, where is your sting? (1 Corinthians 15:55)

While there are three critical events uniquely expressive of Jesus' life, they must be appreciated as intricately unified in what they express. Each of them is first and foremost expressive of the love that is God. Each of them contains messages for us who must meditate on them and seek to uncover what they mean for us and our lives. For viewed together or viewed individually they are calls to humanity to embrace humility, to accept self offering as the way of love, and the supreme message that we must serve each other in imitation of our God who has served us.

In this way the life of Jesus from birth to death and ultimately His victory over death, cannot be parsed as a method for discovering the one central defining event. Jesus' life must be taken in its totality as the supreme mystery of love, generosity, service and sacrifice. St. John's Gospel provides an additional example of the centrality of service as a dimension of the love Jesus was to teach right up to His own death.

It was just before the Passover Feast. Jesus knew that the time had come for him to leave this world and go to the Father. Having loved his own who were in the world, he now showed them the full extent of his love.
The evening meal was being served, and the devil had already prompted Judas Iscariot, son of Simon, to betray Jesus. Jesus knew that the Father had put all things under his power, and that he had come from God and was returning to God; so he got up from the meal, took off his outer clothing, and wrapped a towel around

his waist. After that, he poured water into a basin and began to wash his disciples' feet, drying them with the towel that was wrapped around him...

When he had finished washing their feet, he put on his clothes and returned to his place. "Do you understand what I have done for you?" he asked them. "You call me 'Teacher' and 'Lord,' and rightly so, for that is what I am. Now that I, your Lord and Teacher, have washed your feet, you also should wash one another's feet. I have set you an example that you should do as I have done for you. I tell you the truth, no servant is greater than his master, nor is a messenger greater than the one who sent him. Now that you know these things, you will be blessed if you do them. (John 13: 1-6, 12-18)

While this scene in the Gospel of St. John replaces the last supper offering of bread and wine in the synoptic gospels, St. John has captured the essence in this most intimate sharing. Jesus, having shared the Passover feast with his closest disciples girds his waist with a towel and proceeds to wash their feet. This is yet another inversion of what seems right and seemly. As always, however, it is through turning the expected on its head that Jesus makes his point. Clearly in this case the point is focused on what is essential if one wishes to be His follower.

It was not enough that he knew what was about to transpire as a result of the betrayal of one of those for whom he gave such love. In washing their feet, Jesus becomes the servant and as the servant He expresses the profundity of love. Through embracing the most menial of tasks, Jesus expresses the necessary posture of love. True love cannot be understood in a world of master and slave, king and vassal, lord and serf, only from the perspective of children of God and the egalitarian model this proclaims. His actions thus make clear once again the truth that the only thing that can give one a stature above another is through assuming an inferior position of service.

It is also interesting to juxtapose this foot washing episode with Jesus' acceptance of an invitation to dine with Simon the Pharisee.

> Now one of the Pharisees invited Jesus to have dinner with him, so he went to the Pharisee's house and reclined at the table. When a woman who had lived a sinful life in that town learned that Jesus was eating at the Pharisee's house, she brought an alabaster jar of perfume, and as she stood behind him at his feet weeping, she began to wet his feet with her tears. Then she wiped them with her hair, kissed them and poured perfume on them. When the Pharisee who had invited him saw this, he said to himself, "If this man were a prophet, he would know who is touching him and what kind of woman she is—that she is a sinner." Jesus answered him, "Simon, I have something to tell you."
>
> "Tell me, teacher," he said. "Two men owed money to a certain moneylender. One owed him five hundred denarii, and the other fifty. Neither of them had the money to pay him back, so he canceled the debts of both. Now which of them will love him more?" Simon replied, "I suppose the one who had the bigger debt canceled."
>
> "You have judged correctly," Jesus said. Then he turned toward the woman and said to Simon, "Do you

see this woman? I came into your house. You did not give me any water for my feet, but she wet my feet with her tears and wiped them with her hair. You did not give me a kiss, but this woman, from the time I entered, has not stopped kissing my feet. You did not put oil on my head, but she has poured perfume on my feet. (Luke 7: 36-49)

This quotation contains layers of meaning. For our purposes, it is another occasion where the act of foot washing comes up, but in this case as that which is not provided. At its most simple this scenario is a magnificent description of love; not the expression of love from Simon, the host, but from a sinful women.

There are three major points critical for our reflection. The first point is the lack of judgment from Jesus for the sinful women or Simon, the Pharisee. In fact, the only judgments come from Simon, who has labeled the women as sinful and his questions of Jesus' veracity as a prophet due to His apparent obliviousness of who attends to him. Point two is Jesus' singular focus on service as the manifestation of love. Simon's lack of love is revealed in what he does not do and the sinful women's abundance of love is revealed in what she cannot but do. Point three is Jesus' complete rejection of any meaningful distinction between Simon and this woman. Simon sees distinctions as essential. Simon sees himself as a respected Pharisee, a generous person who has opened his house and prepared a meal for Jesus and his disciples and ultimately as a man worthy of judging Jesus and this woman. Simon and Jesus thus are placed in stark juxtaposition, Jesus the foot washer, the servant and Simon the judge.

Once again, Jesus demonstrates that service is not for the self, but for the other and that no act of service should be seen as too menial for us. This is stated directly and emphatically in the Gospel of St. Mark,

> And he sat down and called the twelve. And he said to them, "If anyone would be first, he must be last of all and servant of all." (Mark 9:35)

Standing back from these initial reflections on Jesus, the question of who He was and the reality of this unparalleled example of His core message, the outline of the nature of service can begin to emerge for us. Service begins by a re-orientation of the self from one of ego-centricity to one of being open and attuned to the larger wonder and opportunity of self expression. In the language we have been using up to now, this entails the willed realignment of our individual vitality from being internally focused on the protecting of my own needs, wants, desires to a new focus on the world seen from the perspective of love, which is the willed desire to see as God sees.

This is the radical choice of trust and faith which enables us to set aside our deep craving to control life and to accept life as it is made clear to us. By thus embracing our inner vulnerability we have the opportunity to see others in a new way. For only in this way can we appreciate their existential fear and vulnerability as being that of our own. In this shared realization, we become humbled and no longer oblivious to the suffering or need of the other for whom we share such an intimately common reality. In coming to embrace our commonality, which cannot be covered over in fine vesture, we can begin to tear down the walls between us that make your experiences invisible to me and mine to you.

It is only when we can truly perceive ourselves and others not as foreigners, but as neighbors, as defined by Jesus, can we hope to let go of our ego-centric and self distorted ways of being. For seeing the world and oneself as God sees it, makes it impossible to be arrogant, self promoting, stingy or mean spirited. This world view also reveals the utter sacrilege of manipulation, indifference and an unwillingness to respond to the needs of another.

God's continued giving is made explicit in the love and the generosity of Jesus expressed in His life as well as His teachings. It is a love focused not on the self, but on others. No matter their state, their lowly position within society, or their past, Jesus embraced all of them. He even noticed the most obscure such as Zacchaeus who was small of stature and had to wedge himself in a tree in the hope that he might catch sight of the man many were calling the Messiah. Jesus repeatedly taught the priorities of life, which sit in stark juxtaposition with those of our modern western society.

> When the Son of Man comes in his glory, and all the angels with him, he will sit on his throne in heavenly glory. All the nations will be gathered before him, and he will separate the people one from another as a shepherd separates the sheep from the goats. He will put the sheep on his right and the goats on his left.
> Then the King will say to those on his right, 'Come, you who are blessed by my Father; take your inheritance, the kingdom prepared for you since the creation of the world. For I was hungry and you gave me

something to eat, I was thirsty and you gave me
something to drink, I was a stranger and you invited me
in, I needed clothes and you clothed me, I was sick and
you looked after me, I was in prison and you came to
visit me.'(Matthew 25: 31-37)

A better description of a life of service would be hard to
find. It is both simple and direct. Unfortunately, this simplicity
can be a trap for persons truly desiring to live the life presented
by Jesus. The issue is, as always, the fundamental interior
orientation required of the individual as the necessary
prerequisite of the complete and fully integrated and authentic
source of actions, which are expressive of the persons Jesus is
calling us to strive to be. Jesus' focus is always on both the
interior motivation of a person and then the actions which
follow on from them. He is most concerned, however, to move
humanity from the empty legalism of His day, which was
characterized by hollow and bloodless acts. It is a focus on what
is driving one and thus external actions alone are seldom true
indicators of a right orientation. How frightening is Jesus'
assessment of the Jewish leaders of his day,

Woe to you, teachers of the law and Pharisees, you
hypocrites! You are like whitewashed tombs, which
look beautiful on the outside but on the inside are full of
dead men's bones and everything unclean. (Mathew
23: 27)

What makes the above quotation so terrifying is the fear we
each should have that this ever be said of us. Pretence is so
much easier than authenticity, seeming rather than truly being.
The issue is that the motivators of actions are never as obvious
as the actions themselves. While the above quotation from

Matthew seeks to focus us on right actions, as always these actions must evolve from the right place within the heart to be truly expressive of what Jesus is striving for. If not, then we too are merely whitewashed tombs.

The disposition of service is by its very nature comprised of supporting attributes. Service requires that the ego not be placed at the center of our consciousness. For only then can we be open and attuned to others. Once this orientation of openness and awareness is attained, it makes possible the capacity to present oneself as a gift to the other. Making oneself a gift entails responding to what one perceives as the good of the other. From this it is clear that generosity is another essential aspect of a life of service. The New Testament story of the Good Samaritan is most illustrative of this view:

> On one occasion an expert in the law stood up to test Jesus. "Teacher," he asked, "what must I do to inherit eternal life?"
>
> "What is written in the Law?" he replied. "How do you read it?"
>
> He answered: "'Love the Lord your God with all your heart and with all your soul and with all your strength and with all your mind'; and, 'Love your neighbor as yourself.'"
>
> "You have answered correctly," Jesus replied. "Do this and you will live."
>
> But he wanted to justify himself, so he asked Jesus, "And who is my neighbor?"
>
> In reply Jesus said: "A man was going down from Jerusalem to Jericho, when he fell into the hands of robbers. They stripped him of his clothes, beat him and went away, leaving him half dead. A priest happened to

be going down the same road, and when he saw the man, he passed by on the other side. So too, a Levite, when he came to the place and saw him, passed by on the other side. But a Samaritan, as he traveled, came where the man was; and when he saw him, he took pity on him. He went to him and bandaged his wounds, pouring on oil and wine. Then he put the man on his own donkey, took him to an inn and took care of him. The next day he took out two silver coins and gave them to the innkeeper. 'Look after him,' he said, 'and when I return, I will reimburse you for any extra expense you may have.'(Luke 10:25-36)

In this classic tale, Jesus is said to be the object of testing by the scribe, i.e. he is being "set-up". Upon asking his somewhat simple question, the scribe is told that only the love of God, which is the correct focus of one's being and expressive of one's essence can gain one the truth that is eternal. The scribe is then given a second directive that is required for his achieving this objective: he must love his neighbor as himself. What is critical in this pericope is that Jesus does not merely ask the scribe to love God, but to love Him with his entire being. It is this kind of love which places love's object at the center of one's being, pushing aside one's ego. It is a love that chooses to see as God sees and to value as God values. It is not a disposition that just happens or that results from the expression of our natures without the active participation of our individual wills. Like most things which are important in our lives, it requires our awareness and our choice.

Even at this stage, the cost of loving God with all one's heart, soul and mind requires a sacrifice. It requires the sacrifice of allowing oneself to be open to the uncertainties of life and to embrace life with an orientation of trust. Its most costly requirement is that we actually embrace reality, and accept the fact that real life is beyond our control. It requires that we lay back as we stand in the rushing flow of the river of life and let it carry us, never quite sure where we shall find ourselves or what we shall encounter, but certain of the unquestionable love of God.

The second aspect of what the scribe must do is to "…love one's neighbor as one's self." The true message is hidden in the concatenating of these two commands, for the first calls one to place God at the core of one's being as its very life energy, orientation and value of the self and then says that one should love one's neighbor as this God centered self. So who is the self that is the object of this love? It is the other as God, the source of life, truth, perspective and service.

The remainder of the pericope merely demonstrates the ramifications of not having one's ego-self set aside and allowing God into one's core. For placing God at the center of who we are does not guarantee that each of us will be saints or perfect, rather that we will have an orientation that has the fullness of being at its center. It enables anyone courageous enough to choose this way of living to be aware, to be a person who sees with both one's eyes and one's heart. It requires the person who chooses this way of being to be vulnerable, not merely from the perspective of the self and those one cares for, but even more essentially vulnerable to the totality of life which is exposed as the context in which our beings are possible.

Ultimately, Jesus lays before us both the Levite and the Priest, both respected members of the community and both representatives of God himself. It is important to note that Jesus does not dwell very long on either individual. He neither sets up their particular dispositions that day or whether they are particularly evil or good men. He also never judges them, but lets the pericope speak for itself. It is very possible that one or both were in a hurry to do some critical work. Jesus never presents this as essential. Their passing by the man in distress merely shows that their concerns—whether they be for time, or their fear of getting involved, or even their potential fear of being infected by religious un-cleanliness—are not considered essential and thus sufficient reason to disregard their fellow human being. All these good (and maybe not-so-good) rationales for seeing and not responding are not presented, for they are not considered valid reasons for passing by another human being in need.

For Jesus, the essential focus is always the human person. No excuse, no concern or worry can ever abrogate our requirement to love each person with whom we come face to face. In Jesus' world-view we are each other's brothers and sisters and nothing is more important than the person who needs our help, our notice and our choice to serve.

The Samaritan was an example of a man looked down upon by the Jewish people and from whom little would be expected. It is, however, this Samaritan who reveals a self that is not held captive by ego demands and who has the internal calm and orientation from which one's sight is opened and the possibility of empathy and generosity are positioned as the basis for the courage to act. The Samaritan sets aside whatever might be pressing upon him, for his focus is on the individual he discovers in need. He then acknowledges the irrefutable truth that each human being is worth more than any possible competing element for our attention. The Samaritan, who fully accepts his vocation, is the self who hears and responds to the call to be a self offering to the world. The Samaritan represents the individual who grasps his essential purpose, which is to be available to serve anyone perceived as in need. This story drives home the centrality of the human call to be gifts of service and love to each other.

Jesus' message, reiterated throughout the Gospels, is a message of the unquestionable sanctity of the human person. No matter if the individual is a Pharisee, Scribe, Greek member of the Sanhedrin, a harlot, tax collector or even a member of the Roman occupying force, each is offered Jesus' attention, concern and love. The often-used metaphor of the shepherd and the sheep presents Jesus as the one willing to lay down His life for us his sheep. Jesus' entire willed existence, which is aligned with that of his Father's will, was to both demonstrate a life of service and love and an undaunted desire to reveal this same orientation as that of His Father.

> When they had finished eating, Jesus said to Simon Peter, "Simon son of John, do you truly love me more than these?"
> "Yes, Lord," he said, "you know that I love you."
> Jesus said, "Feed my lambs."
> Again Jesus said, "Simon son of John, do you truly love me?"
> He answered, "Yes, Lord, you know that I love you."
> Jesus said, "Take care of my sheep."
> The third time he said to him, "Simon son of John, do you love me?"

Peter was hurt because Jesus asked him the third time, "Do you love me?" He said, "Lord, you know all things; you know that I love you."

Jesus said, "Feed my sheep." (John 21:15-18)

The above conversation, which follows the resurrection, is most often discussed from the perspective of Jesus commissioning Peter to lead His church on earth. For our purposes, this wonderful exchange has layers of meaning which can enrich our reflection on service. In singling out Peter for this set of three very pointed exchanges, Jesus offers him an opportunity to re-establish his intimate connection with Jesus after his three-fold denial. For if indeed Peter is being called to the unique role of taking on the position of shepherd, which clearly had been Jesus' role, Peter is being told that he must now be the servant of all. In Jesus' commissioning of Peter, he is told twice to feed His lambs and once to take care of them. Not long before, Jesus taught His disciples the much deeper meaning of feeding within the context of His messages and ministry.

I am the living bread that came down from heaven. If anyone eats of this bread, he will live forever. This bread is my flesh, which I will give for the life of the world."

Then the Jews began to argue sharply among themselves, "How can this man give us his flesh to eat?"

Jesus said to them, "I tell you the truth, unless you eat the flesh of the Son of Man and drink his blood; you have no life in you. Whoever eats my flesh and drinks my blood has eternal life, and I will raise him up at the last day. For my flesh is real food and my blood is real drink. Whoever eats my flesh and drinks my blood remains in me, and I in him. Just as the living Father sent me and I live because of the Father, so the one who feeds on me will live because of me. This is the bread that came down from heaven. Your forefathers ate manna and died, but he who feeds on this bread will live forever. (John 6:51-58)

With the above passage in mind, the command to Peter, repeated twice, to "feed my sheep" is placed in the proper context of first ensuring the centrality of the Eucharist. The Eucharist, both then and now, is the unique expression of the Christian community, as well as the joy, unity and mutual concern of love offered freely to each other in our daily acts. For it is the singularly unique method of maintaining and deepening the intimacy of the shared essence of Jesus made present in and by the communion of believers. Later in the church's development, the central place of the agape meal as a celebration and renewing of our connection with Christ through word and sacrament became an essential expression of the faith community.

Secondarily, the command to "Feed my sheep" can be understood in the larger context of commanding Peter to establish, maintain and protect the communion of believers, so that each member is provided the optimal milieu in which to discern, develop and express their unique gifts for the nurturing, service and redemption of the whole. In this way, feeding is the ongoing uncovering of the meanings that must orient each believer's life, in their specific ways of being and acting. In this command made to Peter to feed Jesus' sheep is the charge to nurture and bring to fruition the gifts of the Holy Spirit in each member of the community who in service to all is called to continually engender ongoing spiritual acts of service, generosity and love.

Jesus' last command to Peter is to "take care of my sheep". As always, our spiritual beings are based on our human natures and thus, for His sheep to be properly shepherded, they must be provided the many ongoing needs and requirements that are basic to our human nature. In making this command, Jesus both acknowledges our human dimension as not incidental and highlights the truth that, if we cannot serve each other at this very basic shared level, it is highly improbable that we will rightly serve each other spiritually.

It is with this in mind that the two reflections (the first on our human nature and this on a framework in which human morality exposes its fullness) which we have been sharing with the larger community are being written. We are each being called to re-embrace our identities and our capacities to transform ourselves with the grace of God already freely provided. It is only through our complete acceptance and understanding of our interdependence on each other as the required condition of redemption and salvation as well as the basis for our hope for better days for our children.

Intertwined with these themes is an appreciation of both the individual dignity of each human person and the critical nature of the community as both the necessary prerequisite for authentic human development and the requirement for the evolution of a true Christian community from our scattered and broken societies. For Jesus the community he discovered in the formal Jewish religious society preoccupied by law and sacrifice and under the thumb of Roman oppression provided a stark contrast to the community He still calls forth from all men and women of good will. For Jesus community or *communio*, which is so much more richly understood as communion, necessitated the full embrace of each human being as equally a child of God and thus worthy of love and service. *Communio*, communion and Eucharist as has been demonstrated, each inform the other such that they are all necessary and sufficient conditions for reality as a whole.

Communion as the word often used by Christian communities to identify what one receives as the outcome of the liturgical reenactment of the Last Supper is intimately united with the actual community of believers. Jesus is made present, sacramentally, but even more in the ongoing lives lived in consistent witness of His messages and personal example. which effect this mysterious transformation of mere bread and wine into the Eucharistic presence of Jesus.

After the rediscovery of Aristotle in the west the church was faced both with a tremendous opportunity and potential threat. Most of the Church's teachings up to this point were derived from the earlier Platonic school of thought and the concepts that this school was able to provide early theologians for expressing their faith. Now with the re-introduction of Aristotle, who was not only Plato's student, but his greatest challenger and the slow translations of Aristotle's ideas into Latin, new and in some cases better ways of describing theological truths began to emerge. One key area significantly affected was the articulation of a way of understanding the mystery of the Eucharist.

The idea that during the liturgy the bread and wine of Jesus were central elements in making Christ present was a solid doctrine of orthodox faith. What this meant was not so easily articulated. Over time, the church had clearly denied the physicalist view that the consecration actually changed the bread into Jesus' flesh and the wine to Jesus' blood (at a cellular level). The issue was that identifying false teachings was easier than trying to explain a mystery.

Aristotle's *Metaphysics* was central to the Church's ability to develop a positive statement about the transformation that took place when the priest consecrated the bread and wine. In order to grasp this, a brief description of Aristotle's belief in the nature of all reality is required.

For Aristotle everything found in the world of our experience, both animate and inanimate things, are comprised of two components. The first, is the matter (sometimes referred to as its substance) of which the thing was composed. Let's use an example of a table. The table we are looking at is made of solid oak. In Aristotelian terms, the matter or substance of the table is oak. The second element of anything that can be experienced is described by its form, or more colloquially the pattern in which its matter is manifest. Using our example of the table, the form that the oak has taken is that of a table.

Aristotle took the ideas of form and matter and used them as descriptive terms for any earthly reality. Form is the pattern that matter takes. It does so in this world of our experience. As a philosopher of this world who was keenly interested in classifying the phenomenon that he saw all around him, Aristotle showed that each natural phenomenon was composed of these very two realities matter and form.

Applying this methodology to the Eucharist, Aquinas would use Aristotle's mode of classification and attempt to explain the miracle of how Jesus is made present in the celebration of the Eucharist. Aquinas accepted the unleavened wheat as the matter or substance of the bread. As a result of the consecration, Aquinas postulated that the substance or matter of the bread remained just as it was prior to the consecration. What had changed was the form of the bread. For as a result of the consecration the form of the bread became the body of Christ. In the same way the wine, as fermented grapes, is the matter. As a result of the consecration the matter of the wine remained unchanged, and once again only its form was altered into the blood of Christ. This answered the physicalist heresy that held that the post consecrated bread and wine were now the flesh and blood of Jesus in all ways. Aquinas' explanation was given the moniker of transubstantiation.

Over the centuries, there have been numerous attempts by theologians to articulate what occurs in the miracle of the agape meal. I shall only present one, for it makes sense within the anthropology and moral framework being posited. This theory is called transignification.

Using this framework, it is possible to reexamine the miracle of the Eucharist as the act of the Christian community, inclusive of the presider and the people of God. The concept of transignification, which has not been accepted as an appropriate explanation for what happens in the miracle of the agape meal is built on the reality of the efficacious will. The human faith community present at the agape meal transform the reality of the bread and wine through their faith which alters the reality of the bread and wine through their altered faith-viewed perceptions and meanings. Just as our willed meanings can alter life's experiences, in this case, we as a united community of believers have affected a miracle by making Christ present in a fundamentally unique way. This transformation is the result of the communal willed meaning as expressive of the Church as *communio*. Thus, just as the meaning we give to a situation truly creates the experience we have, so now both our individual and communal willed choice of meaning has a real manifestation in the mystery of the Eucharist. In this very special way, we as individuals and as community are both the shared participants in the bringing of Christ into our presence and the direct beneficiaries.

The mystery of the presence of Christ in the Eucharist has, of course, been a sticking point of theological dispute over centuries. It may be good to remember that the essential element for which all theological explanations search is an understanding of the ways in which the risen Lord is present; as expressed in the, "Alleluia! Christ is risen!" Too much theological parsing can do as much to obscure as to reveal him. During the reign of Mary Tudor, a staunch Roman Catholic, her half sister, Elizabeth was quizzed on her understanding of the presence of Christ in the Eucharist. Her answer, though politically careful, is a classically beautiful statement of trusting faith in the risen Christ:

Christ was the word that spake it.
He took the bread and break it.
And what his words did make it
That I believe and take it.

As we have discovered, the free choice of our capacity to give meaning to every reality, including ourselves, is a fundamental truth which each of us must come to terms with.

This facet of ourselves has exposed us to the fact that people, things, situations and indeed our very selves are indistinct realities. Without our giving these perceptions texture through how we experience them is what is meant by the meanings in which we clothe them.

In this way we have come to appreciate our human natures as both receptive and creative. This fact is crucial, for we have never postulated that the world is just the meanings any one of us gives it, but most essentially the mixture of both the individual meanings and the meanings which we as the community accept.

To the degree that we are able to take this shared reality with us from our places of worship and continue to offer ourselves as expressions of the unparalleled gift of God to us in communion we continue to be communion for each other.

CHAPTER 6

Serviam—The Human Dimensions

Where the discussion of *non-serviam* required an in-depth reflection on the role of the ego, the focus in this section concerning "service" will require an in-depth reflection on the role of human mortality, humility and generosity as essential aspects of a life of service.

The fact that human existence is bounded on two sides, one being birth and the other death has more significance to our lives than just as the two framing events. The common boundaries of all humanity bring with them the undeniable unity of the human condition. No human can escape either border. Together they stand like existential book-ends not merely framing every human life, but creating the context in which human living occurs. This pre-condition of human existence pronounces the fundamental equality among all human beings, of low and high estate alike. Human life, which occurs in between these events, is a mixture of circumstance, fate, choice and will. To fail to appreciate the impinging nature of humanity's container is to fail to grasp a fundamental element that shapes the nature of humanity itself.

The most basic question about life's meaning is thrust upon us as a result of life's finitude. It is not merely a philosophical pondering, but a question that emerges from one's very soul.

For the reality that imposes its full weight on each of us is not the fact that people die; it is the realization that it is I who shall die. With this realization of my end and the shared reality that it is the same for all humans, one is forced to consider what happens within the brackets of birth and death with much more seriousness. As not only conscious, but reflective beings, humans are forced to confront life's meaning or lack thereof, again not theoretically, but specifically as one's own.

The resulting effect of our mortality on the existential reality of living is thus profound. Many thinkers, such as the existentialist Camus, looked at life and saw in it an inherent absurdity. To accept life's all-too-few moments of joy, as well as the periods of great sorrow and suffering only to end as food for worms seemed to Camus at best a cruel joke.

> Beauty is unbearable, drives us to despair, offering us for a minute the glimpse of an eternity that we should like to stretch out over the whole of time.
> (Albert Camus, http://quotewords.com/quotes/Albert_Camus.html)

Others have postulated that the assertion of absurdity is to miss the point entirely. For many, it is this framed context resulting from our mortality that necessitates the need to discover, create and give meaning to life. It is this which makes human existence so very different than the existence of the other creatures with which we share this world.

> Unlike man, animals, so to speak, live without knowing death. The individual animal enjoys fully the immutability of its gender, being conscious of itself

only as an immortal being. (Arthur Schopenhauer, *The World as Will and Representation*, Dover, NY, 1966)

While death is a fact of all life, it is a unique reality for humanity, as our mortality is, and cannot fail to be, an object of our reflective concern. It is our mortality that provides the very foundation for the development of our coming to discover what is real versus what is mere illusion. It is the context from which humans are provided the stage upon which we have been given both the capacity and power to create ourselves and our world. It is the context which thrusts an existential imperative on us to make more of our lives than mere existence. It ensures that this challenge is actually accepted and met, but it makes it such that, no matter how we choose to face our lives, we do so with an acute awareness.

It is with this understanding that Shakespeare reveals the depth of his appreciation of human existence.

All the world's a stage,
And all the men and women merely players;
They have their exits and their entrances,
And one man in his time plays many parts,
His acts being seven ages. At first, the infant,
Mewling and puking in the nurse's arms.
Then the whining schoolboy, with his satchel
And shining morning face, creeping like snail
Unwillingly to school. And then the lover,
Sighing like furnace, with a woeful ballad
Made to his mistress' eyebrow. Then a soldier,
Full of strange oaths and bearded like the bard,
Jealous in honor, sudden and quick in quarrel,
Seeking the bubble reputation

Even in the canon's mouth. And then the justice,
In fair round belly with good capon lined,
With eyes severe and beard of formal cut,
Full of wise saws and modern instances;
And so he plays his part. The sixth age shifts
Into the lean and slippered pantaloon
With spectacles on nose and pouch on side;
His youthful hose, well saved, a world too wide
For his shrunk shank, and his big manly voice,
Turning again toward childish treble, pipes
And whistles in his sound. Last scene of all,
That ends this strange eventful history,
Is second childishness and mere oblivion,
Sans teeth, sans eyes, sans taste, sans everything.
(*As You Like It*, 2. 7. 139-167)

As so poetically articulated, human life is anything but the progression of one listless ordinary moment to the next. Each of these "acts", which seem to be common across humanity are situational episodes open to our capacities to expand and identify new facets of our identities. As such these acts are our opportunities to choose to be at a level of existence and expression, which we have avoided up to this point. The quality of our entrances and exits are thus ours to embrace. Regardless of the choices we make and the quality of our life, we will perform our chosen roles; we will act out our parts at each inflection point and, most critical of all, we will do so, as with all plays, in a constant movement toward the final scene.

The above quote could no more beautifully state the reality of the major stages of life and our ultimate end, death. These phases of human existence each express our brief process of coming into the fullness of our strength and then reverting in an almost cyclical manner to our fragile neediness sans (without) teeth, eyes, taste and ultimately our life. Shakespeare is juxtaposing the focus of human existence at each of its phases as requiring their proper orientation through a conscious acceptance of death which seems to brood over life itself.

Martin Heidegger, the somewhat infamous philosopher of the twentieth century, remarked that (and I am paraphrasing) a precondition for an individual to discover and live life authentically requires that one face the reality of one's own impending death. At first sight this may seem a rather morose thought, but upon further investigation it shows itself to contain truths essential to our right orientation to life.

Mahatma Gandhi also shared this appreciation of the acceptance of one's death as a central part of ensuring a more rich way of living as demonstrated in his quote: "Live as if you were to die tomorrow. Learn as if you were to live forever."

Death as the universal experience of all humans is the end of life as we know it. For many people the reality of death is not only something to be kept as far from one's consciousness as possible, but it also evokes significant anxiety and trepidation. It is therefore necessary to separate the two main aspects of death in order for us to discover the jewel at its core, removing the source of anxiety which can occlude our reflection. The aspect of death that focuses on the process of dying is not what will be reflected upon, for it is neither universal nor predictable and thus has little to offer. It is often this experience of death that is what most people are anxious about.

Our focus shall be on death as the cessation of life. It is this aspect of death that is universal and predictable. Reflecting on this shared event can provide significant material for better understanding our lives and our vocation to service, which is at the heart of our moral framework.

As with a play, the actor may be given a great part, beautiful costumes and a role that would be the envy of anyone. The reality is that the actor does not take on her role as her real identity. Nor does she accept her costumes in all their beauty as her possessions. Each player knows that who they are in this play is only for the period of the play. Their positions, their assumed wealth or power are all a fiction that ends as the curtain descends. What a grand analogy to human life, but unfortunately something which is realized by a few.

Human mortality plays an essential existential role in the life of every human being regardless of our conscious awareness of this fact. Death brings human life to its close. In this sense, death positions our lives as conscious and reflective beings with the capability of infusing life with a purpose born of reflection and meditation.

No, no, go not to Lethe, neither twist
Wolf's-bane, tight-rooted, for its poisonous wine;
Nor suffer thy pale forehead to be kiss'd
By nightshade, ruby grape of Proserpine;
Make not your rosary of yew-berries,
Nor let the beetle, nor the death-moth be
Your mournful Psyche, nor the downy owl
A partner in your sorrow's mysteries;
For shade to shade will come too drowsily,
And drown the wakeful anguish of the soul.
But when the melancholy fit shall fall
Sudden from heaven like a weeping cloud,

That fosters the droop-headed flowers all,
And hides the green hill in an April shroud;
Then glut thy sorrow on a morning rose,
Or on the rainbow of the salt sand-wave,
Or on the wealth of globed peonies;
Or if thy mistress some rich anger shows,
Emprison her soft hand, and let her rave,
And feed deep, deep upon her peerless eyes.
She dwells with Beauty—Beauty that must die;
And Joy, whose hand is ever at his lips
Bidding adieu; and aching Pleasure nigh,
Turning to poison while the bee-mouth sips:
Ay, in the very temple of Delight
Veil'd Melancholy has her sovran shrine,
Though seen of none save him whose strenuous tongue
Can burst Joy's grape against his palate fine;
His soul shalt taste the sadness of her might,
And be among her cloudy trophies hung.
(*Ode to Melancholy*, John Keats
http://www.bartleby.com/101/628.html)

The above *Ode* by John Keats beautifully ties together the experiences of the richest pleasures of life with their intensity, which is the result of their relationship to their intimate passing. For melancholy, upon which Keats is reflecting, is the queen whose reign exists between the sweet joy of the ruptured grape and its dissipation, or between the perfect wonder of a flowers bloom which at the very instant of its greatest beauty gives way to the quiet almost imperceptible wilt, which shall take it away.

Without death, the proper intensity associated with a life embraced to experience all its wonders can be overlooked. The importance of each moment as the only real moment in which

I am and in which I can discover myself, others and God can be blurred without this prerequisite attentiveness. This is true due to the fact that without death my innumerable moments would be assumed to run on eternally without any sense of finality, and without this finality the purpose of one's life would be diluted, at best.

To make this point clear, consider, if you will, a football game. Imagine what the game would be like if at half time the referees were to announce to the players and fans that this game would go on forever. While we may have thought this true of many an actual game, we mean something much more real here. As you might imagine, soon the playing would become less intense, less focused. Finally, it would dissolve into what might resemble a pre game practice session and then ultimately many of the players would probably leave the field and go home. If, on the other hand, I were to postulate another football game, where before the game commenced the coaches announced that this game would be played with unique and specific rules only applicable to it. As usual, at the whistle blow the game would start. The only difference would be that the game could end at any point. The game could end prior to traditional half time or even sometime after half-time. In fact, the game could commence and continue without end. In this scenario, one can imagine a focus and intensity in the players that would be quite different from the aforementioned described scenario.

In this way one can see how the end of a game infuses the playing of the game with meaning and purpose. While life is certainly not a game, the same dynamics are involved. The major difference is that humans have the ability willfully to blind themselves from the reality of the end of their lives as an impending possibility at any moment. It is not the intent of this reflection on death to ask one to drape black bunting around each moment. Life is not meant to be without joy and wonder. What this reflection is trying to convey is that we should never take the trappings of life too seriously. We are mere borrowers and users of life's many gifts. As such we should always be careful of being like the foolish actor who allows his role to become all too real and thus looks the fool after the curtain falls. Or like the character of Macbeth whose ultimate success in achieving his earthly goals ultimately pronounces its judgment in light of life's end and the truth it reveals.

To-morrow, and to-morrow, and to-morrow, creeps in this petty pace from day to day, to the last syllable of recorded time; And all our yesterdays have lighted fools The way to dusty death. Out, out, brief candle! Life's but a walking shadow; a poor player, that struts and frets his hour upon the stage, and then is heard no more: it is a tale told by an idiot, full of sound and fury, signifying nothing. (*Macbeth* Act 5, Scene 5, 19-28)

How sad and telling, this utterance says so much about the man, himself, and the ramifications of his limitless self absorption and ambition. It is the resulting murderous life which drove him to such despair. This quotation so often memorized by young students of literature, makes explicit the tight connection between how one lives life and how the chosen ways of living and one's actions return their blessings or curses onto the soul of their author. For Macbeth, whose life has been the single-minded clawing for self promotion and power, and death now reveals his folly and proclaims him an idiot.

This rather lengthy reflection on death has highlighted many essential facets of a true life of service. Initially it has exposed the somewhat obvious truth that seems to escape many of us, and that is the reality that all of us are essentially the same. Death makes clear the foolishness of the many preoccupations that fill our lives, often at the expense of the joy of life itself. The service that Jesus proposed as the essential call of the highest in society to be offered to the lowest is thus in the light of our human nature merely the truth hidden behind our childlike games.

> I am the good shepherd; the good shepherd lays down His life for the sheep…Greater love has no one than this that one lay down his life for his friends. (John 10:11 & 15:13)

The above quotations make clear that the ultimate gift of one being to another is the free gift of their life for the benefit of the other. Most of us assume that this gift must be our physical death. The truth is that, in every act of selfless service in which I generously offer my time, my aid, or my attention to another, I am offering my life. For the truth being made explicit by this reflection is that any moment offered to another is the ultimate gift of a moment of my life never retrievable and yet incapable of being better spent. It is a moment gone and never to return and in this very real sense it is thus the offering of my life. The secret of Jesus' consistent call and command is that we start by seeing our small acts of service in just this way, as the giving of our lives for each other.

Another aspect of a life orientation of service necessitates the virtue of humility. This is not self abnegation or a predilection for self deprecation. It is the healthy appreciation of oneself as a creature among creatures. It is but another aspect of the lesson learned through our reflection on our own shared mortality. Both pride and its opposite humility are critical elements of human reality. As the following quote demonstrates these two opposites have been a central part of human mythology for many an age as well.

It was pride that changed angels into devils; it is humility that makes men as angels. (Augustine, *Confessions*, Penguin, London, 1961.)

It is the awareness that the lowliest state is but a breath away and that no thing or position or capability that one may be blessed with essentially differentiates one from anyone else and that such things are at best illusory aspects of our shared lives. As stated in Proverbs: "Better it is to be of a humble spirit with the lowly, than to divide the spoil with the proud." (Proverbs 16:19) In short, humility is the internalized realization that we are all creatures and that each person is my brother or sister and I theirs. This highly egalitarian view of humanity is the necessary outcome of a view of creation that stresses no royal families, no favored children, only the all pervasive and universally applied love that is both life giving and life sustaining.

In its essence the truth that is being articulated is the acceptance of the fact that the emperor truly does not have any clothing and that all of the innumerable methods humanity has used in an attempt to draw distinctions between one human and another are just postulated illusory coverings proffered to an always naked dignitary. This humility is the stark awareness that all our delineations which make one person admirable and another ordinary are merely accidentals. This humility is also the constant awareness that no matter how exalted one may be at any moment in time, no one is ever too far from the nakedness and neediness that promises to expose that which brings terror into the minds and hearts of those with means as it demonstrates the truth which is at the heart of us all.

In youth, the strength and vitality of life seems to overflow from the very font of our beings. It often appears that nothing can truly challenge our vigor, and our capacities to express our vitality. Except in those unusual occasions where youth is colored by physical injury, illness or malfunction or in the sad case of the premature death of a parent, sibling or other loved one, few young people have any reason to know death as their own shadow.

It is this reality of our youths that often disposes young people to be overly risky and willing to take chances with their lives of which few adults would dream. It is also this aspect of our early years that can color much of how the young see life, other people and their responsibilities.

Many of the ideas and thoughts of one's elders often appear, from the perspective of the young, as foreign, as if they were the utterances of someone waxing on in another language. In most cases, this is in great part due to the lack of experience associated with youth, especially as it relates to life's fragility. Our western culture has separated, in some cases for very good reason, our elderly from being integral parts of our families. The cost of this has been in great part to exacerbate this situation in which our young people are not offered the needed perspective of the aging and elderly.

At the same time, we live in a culture that eschews death, old age and the infirm themselves. Our western culture is oriented toward eternal youth. Billions of dollars are spent on every sort of promise to hold back aging and the natural signs of its progression. How many products do we hear about daily concerning methods of thwarting the effects of aging as seen in the lines of one's face, the loss of one's hair or its turning grey; once thought to be a sign of wisdom and respect?

Countless messages tell our young not to embrace the flow of their lives with both the limitations and the blessings that accompany each period. Gyms have become the new houses of worship for many. Many of these devotees are not there to embrace methods of maintaining their health, but to reshape their bodies into monuments of youth and strength even when the degree to which some pursue this can be detrimental to their overall health.

Aging and death are no longer appreciated as the natural progression of life with their unique joys and experiences, which should be treasured rather than feared. Nor are the signs of aging that once elicited respect and deference as common as once they were. The wisdom of one who has succeeded in living through the many stages of life is, unfortunately, seldom sought.

This blocking of the process of aging as a natural part of life is a radical distortion. It places youth outside of its right orientation toward maturation and, yes, even death. It reinforces the delusion of immortality in our youth and thus a lack of appreciation that their lives are gifts and their ongoing maturity an ongoing blessing. This reality, which so many seek to escape, of the essential link between life, growing older and ultimately the impermanence that results from the universality of death, is expressed quite beautifully by the Buddha,

> This existence of ours is as transient as autumn clouds. To watch the birth and death of beings is like looking at the movements of a dance. A lifetime is a flash of lightning in the sky. Rushing by, like a torrent down a steep mountain.
> (Berscholz, S. and Kohn, S.C., *The Buddha and His Teachings*, Shambala, Boston, 2003)

And yet, this acceptance of our impermanence and death are essential to our living life to its fullest and our gaining a proper orientation toward life and our own processes of becoming. Once one accepts and integrates the truth of human unfolding as well as the process of aging, only then can this same appreciation be extended to others.

Accepting the reality that I will die, that I am dying, and the truth that this event is as possible for me in the next instant as it is at any instant to follow are formidable aspects of accepting the life that is ours. One cannot accept one's life as truly a gift without accepting the reality that it can end at any time. The rich possibilities of life as a critical beckoning, which have their appropriate time and place and which must be engaged in with all seriousness and deliberation cannot be appreciated without accepting the natural process of life.

Service as a posture of one who respects those who have trodden life's many paths as well as the service offered from the life tested through time and trial to those for whom the bloom of youth has yet to fade is essential. For the elderly owe to the young their wisdom and the young owe to the elderly their ears.

After twenty-years of service as the Bishop of Rome, and in celebration of his life as Bishop and Pope, John Paul II publically shared with the thousands who sought to celebrate with him the very intimate questions which ruminated within him as he faced more clearly the coming end of his life.

I cannot fail to ask myself a few questions today. Have you observed all this? Are you a diligent and watchful teacher of faith in the Church? Have you sought to bring the great work of the Second Vatican Council closer to the people of today? Have you tried to satisfy the expectations of believers within the Church, and the hunger for truth which is felt in the world outside the Church? (Weigel, George, *Witness to Hope*, p.840)

The very willingness of this incredible man to ask these questions of himself at this point in his life and to do so in the full humility of a public celebration is both touching and indicative of a man who saw his life as a life of service and love, both to his flock and to the shepherd that asked him to tend it.

As the quote above verifies most movingly, human mortality is the cornerstone of our appreciation of our lives as equal to all other humans. It is one of the few realities that level all human assessments. Whether these differences are in race, religion, social status, wealth or natural abilities, all these distinctions are erased through the process of aging and death.

Death also acts as the final curtain call that enables the real worth of a life to be judged. As a result death establishes the capacity for one's life to be truly assessed. It provides the finality from which the individual human drama can be understood. In addition, the reality that death happens to me as well as everyone else creates the need to appreciate the lives of others as it does our own lives.

Service as the true offering of myself to another is the outcome of my facing and accepting the shared dignity and sacredness that each human person expresses. It is only with eyes willing to let the heart see that we can move past the repulsive, the dirty and grotesque and, as St. Francis of Assisi was purported to do, embrace the leper as the vessel of God's Spirit. It is with an orientation cleansed of moral judgment that service to all is possible. It is a re-embracing of the ancient tradition of giving alms. This practice was based on the inherent worthiness of each person. It held off concerns for how the alms might be used. The rationale was that in alms giving I was giving my offering to God.

In determining the paths of one's life, one is confronted with a multitude of choices. Each choice will entail a set of meanings and objectives both for the self and for the world. Each of these paths also has imbedded within it particular values. Values are one of the essential artifacts that each of us must confront within the larger constructs of the cultures in which we are formed. In fact, it would not be an over statement to say that values are the most important artifacts that one generation leaves to the next as the foundation upon which humanities forward evolution can be based.

Many will seek out and familiarize themselves with the values which have been identified and cherished as new realizations concerning our lives as community as well as our lives appreciated in the silence of the moon light. For others these values will be rejected artifacts and thus the paths chosen will be in opposition to them. Sometimes this antagonism is merely a phase required by the individual to come to see themselves in a new way and only then integrate new dimensions of their identities as ongoing signs of God's grace. There are other cases where the initial rejection and the emotional vigor surrounding the question of the values of the past will be so strong as to almost ensure that these values will find themselves hard-pressed to reemerge in the lives of these individuals. Service and an orientation of self giving, generosity and an inherent respect for each person are some of the values that are essential to ensuring the ongoing possibility of both civilization and Christianity.

A life of service demands that the only real meanings worthy of human life must be imbued with love, generosity, genuine humility and regard for all other human persons as fellow children of God. A life of service thus requires the acceptance of our lives as gifts and of our vocations to give from the bounty of our giftedness. The life of service is thus the heart of community. Theologically, it is the awareness of each of us as irreplaceable members of the body of Christ. For this reason it is His life that is taken as the way and His life as service that makes one's life of service necessary.

At its center, the life of service is a way of proper self appreciation. It requires that each of us accept and nourish our gifts as well as our limitations. Service is not subjugation or a belittling of the self. It is of necessity an orientation of inner humility, but this humility requires that we appreciate and embrace our individuality as an indicator of the unique reality of all others who stand before us.

God welcomes genuine service, and that is the service of a soul that offers the bare and simple sacrifice of truth; but from false service, the mere display of material wealth, He turns away. (attributed to: Philo of Alexandria)

The above attribution puts the concept of service in a helpful context. It is the genuine gift of the self as a self. In this sense it is more than the sharing of things that are external to the self and thus of questionable meaning to the self. True service is thus the offering of our very selves to each other along with the awareness of the cost of this giving. It is a gift, for one cannot, nor should one wish to, determine how the gift is received or appreciated. In this sense, while it is an actual gift of my time, my company, and my attention it is given both to the actual receiver and to our Lord in the awareness of the tremendous gift he gave to me.

A life of service proffers an entirely different set of criteria for judging the value of one's life than the many alternatives offered by modern society. Worldly attributes of wealth, power, and prestige are replaced by virtues of generosity, self giving and the capacity of seeing all humans as equally deserving of one's notice, respect and response.

By its very nature service requires that one be attuned to the reality which surrounds one and that there be a willing spirit to give of oneself in the face of any person discovered in need.

Service also demands that the sacredness of human life be at the forefront of our consciousness. As a result, this priority guarantees that the other demands on our lives not take precedence over the needs of those with whom we come into contact. Service most significantly colors how we live our lives in that it shapes the way or manner in which we fulfill our many roles as parent, manager, priest, religious, politician or friend. Service is an openness of our senses and our heart to the needs of others. It is an internal commitment to be at the disposal of others with no regard for what it will get us in return. It is, in this way, a true result of the internalization of our commonality with all other human beings.

As we noted, the true acceptance of life, human life, as a process of unfolding and of becoming is in part the embracing of the gift of each moment as the single opportunity to live and to offer ourselves in service to others. As such the predilection for us to judge others and to cut them off is not something worthy of a person true to a life of service. For as I appreciate my life as an evolution, I realize that I have often done things or said things that were unbecoming and thus, just as I am no longer that same person, so might the person who in the past offended me be more than they were at the time of the offence. An orientation of service would thus break down walls and make space for peace and its prerequisite, forgiveness. It is with this in mind that the teaching of Jesus makes sense.

Then Peter approaching asked him, "Lord, if my brother sins against me, how often must I forgive him? As many as seven times?" Jesus answered, "I say to you, not seven times but seventy-seven times." (Matthew 18: 18-20)

If one embraces one's identity as something that is truly dynamic and an ever evolving process how can one truly forgive oneself for past actions and yet be closed to bestowing such generous forgiveness on another. It is within this spirit that I come to appreciate the gift of my life, as the ultimate gift. Only as a result of this realization concerning my own life can I come to feel the same about the life of another. In this way forgiveness of oneself will always precede one's authentic capacity to forgive another. Forgiveness is truly a profound act of service offered to oneself and in like manner to another.

Our existences are such that there is no promise of tomorrow, or even of the next moment. As such we each come to an awareness of the inherent precariousness of life. This realization can lead one to begin to appreciate their days as inherently valuable and requiring one's full attention and openness. There develops in the aware individual the need to live with a passion equal to the irreplaceable moment. With this realization our need is to be like children who can see the wonder, beauty, joy and possibility of life in the smallest of things. We are beckoned to put aside the bleariness of seeing each day as merely the repetition of the ones that have preceded it.

This truth of the wonder and magnificence of the gift of life as well as its inherent sanctity as described most profoundly in a 1995 Encyclical,

> Man is called to a fullness of life which far exceeds the dimensions of his earthly existence, because it consists in sharing the very life of God. The loftiness of this supernatural vocation reveals the greatness and the inestimable value of human life even in its temporal

phase. Life in time, in fact, is the fundamental condition, the initial stage and an integral part of the entire unified process of human existence. It is a process which, unexpectedly and undeservedly, is enlightened by the promise and renewed by the gift of divine life, which will reach its full realization in eternity (cf. 1 Jn 3:1-2). At the same time, it is precisely this supernatural calling which highlights the relative character of each individual's earthly life. After all, life on earth is not an "ultimate" but a "penultimate" reality; even so, it remains a sacred reality entrusted to us, to be preserved with a sense of responsibility and brought to perfection in love and in the gift of ourselves to God and to our brothers and sisters. (Ioannes Paulus PP. II *Evangelium Vitae*, 1995)

A life of service is the proper response of appreciation and acceptance of the wonder of the gift of our lives. This realization removes the distorted sense of entitlement. Instead of the arrogance of entitlement a sense of thankfulness and an acute awareness of the responsibility to use our gifts to further the lot of those not so blessed emerges. A life of service is first a life oriented toward others. It is a denial of the narcissism born from the misguided sense that one's blessings are somehow deserved. In this way service requires one to be open to life in a manner which breaks through the narrowness of self and enables one to experience the vast wonder, awe and beauty of existence from which the context of fully engaging life can reveal a myriad of possibilities. Not only does the perspective of service increase one's awareness of the richness of life and its infinite opportunities for self expression and engagement, but coupled with this appreciation for its preciousness comes a deeper capacity to truly prize each moment as a unique instant for living that might never be repeated. In this way the acceptance of our mortal coil evokes a deep and vast appreciation of our life, of others and the imperative that not a single instant be squandered.

With maturation and openness one soon begins to appreciate that their possessions, their titles, degrees and prestige are no longer expressive of the depth of one's essence or of whom one truly is. If one is poised to hear the message of life, one should also begin to grasp the inherent interconnectedness of each person. The disparities between those who have amassed great fortunes and those without the mere necessities begin to disturb one's sense of justice. At first one is sensitized to the macro-issues of our culture and society, and only slowly do we begin to focus more finely on ourselves and our personal vocation. At this stage, the individual is challenged to be open to and address injustice, hatred, indifference and apathy in their own lives. Many find it very hard to go from the macro truths to the personal vocation, for it is easier to think and speak about the injustice of society, governments, and religious institutions than it is to speak of my own vocation to respond to the apathy, indifference, injustice and selfishness in my own life. It takes great courage to bring these insights to a personal level.

The inner humility which is at the heart of service is derived from the realization that my life is no more meritorious than any other life, or as Jesus put it,

> "...your Father in heaven...makes his sun rise on both evil and good people, and he lets rain fall on the righteous and the unrighteous." (Matthew 5:45)

The true life of service is also a life accepting of suffering as part of the fabric of human existence. Once again it is Jesus who shows us this as an integral part of the way. The crucifixion stands as the supreme pouring out of Himself in His human nature, as an offering for humanity. This facet of his life cannot be isolated from the way He was making explicit to us.

Then Jesus told his disciples, "If anyone would come after me, let him deny himself and take up his cross and follow me. (Matthew 16:24)

The cross, which stands for the willed acceptance of suffering as a part of the human condition stands front and center as a necessary element of the way that Jesus is laying out. It is not a search for pain. It is the acceptance of all the pains and anguish of our lives with a view of making it an offering for those whose sorrow and anguish one cannot even imagine. It is the acceptance of the existential reality of suffering as a genuine part of human existence. It is in part the realization that suffering is part of the process of calling forth all the wondrous attributes of the human person. Without it we would not know compassion, courage, and the potential depths of human dignity. It is also our coming to acknowledge in the most real way possible that our lives are an offering of the purest kind to each other and to God via our capacity to suffer with dignity and courage. For any person's suffering is a cry to the larger community to embrace the one who suffers and to bring all the solace and relief that we can. In this way suffering should never be something done alone. It is the truest test of our embracing a life of service that we seek to be aware and to choose to bring comfort to those who suffer.

In our culture many see suffering as something akin to death and thus to be avoided at all costs; certainly, as it pertains to oneself and equally our lack of comfort in being present to those who suffer. It is often for this reason that many seem incapable of just dwelling with the sufferer. Many of us seek answers to offer the suffering when confronted with it. Many of us can become impatient with those who suffer, as we ourselves are uncomfortable with it.

The sudden death of my father truly opened my eyes to the reality of suffering. Initially, many people came out to express their support for my family and especially my mother. It seemed that the generosity of people was almost too much for one to bear. Once the funeral and the repast were over, it seemed as if the expectation was that we should take a couple of weeks to mourn, but then move on and go back to those things that were central to our lives.

I remember wishing that the custom of wearing a black arm band around one's coat for a year were still in practice. For this very sensitive symbol made anyone with whom one came in contact aware that one was still in that very intense period of mourning and thus communicated a vulnerability probably still being carried within the one who mourned. Our present lack of such symbols demonstrates a complete disregard for the process of mourning and the reality that this healing does take time. Unfortunately, true to our culture in which death is to be kept as far from our consciousness as possible, we both miss another opportunity to embrace those who mourn and thus to bring them the healing balm of communal concern. This lack of symbols associated with death also has the unfortunate effect of allowing each of us to keep this central human reality far from our thoughts.

CHAPTER 7

The Way of Service

This reflection has been an attempt to create a moral framework which would be broad enough to be relevant to our modern times and rich enough to anticipate the many moral scenarios which seem to evolve with increasing speed in these times. It has also explored the audacious desire to discover a method that might be capable of leaving in operation the full richness our human will with its robust existential freedom, as well as its aching responsibilities and culpabilities.

A sound morality is born of a true appreciation of the human person. A morality that does not take the time to articulate a description of human nature would merely float above us as a potentially arbitrary imposition on our humanity. It would seem impossible for us to claim a moral perspective or to establish a moral framework without also discovering humanity's larger purpose and our attempt to embrace it. In this way a morality devoid of a belief posture has always seemed at best merely a shell in search of that which once inhabited it and gave it life. The miracle of human beings, formed with the god-like capacity to reason as well as the ability to know one's self in a way unique from the remainder of creation, is lost without hope of being found if this confluence of capacities and potentialities is considered the result of mere chance. Both our individual and social compasses are inept at finding our true north once bereft of our author.

Modern secular society seems to feel comfortable creating moralities that are built on such things as utility, happiness, success, and the appearance of a social inter-connection only strong enough to be called upon if attacked or threatened in any way. For these reasons, even when certain individuals or societies appear to promulgate moral positions, they often fall upon deaf ears. If modern societies are truly desirous of putting behind them the beliefs that gave substance to their moralities, then they might look to ethics—a principle based, rather than faith based system—as their source for guiding human lives and providing the source of our proper constraints.

This has certainly been tried, but it would be a stretch to say that these ethical positions have been able to express truths buried deep within the human person. Without this ability they neither have the potency to drive humans to grasp their lives as the potentials they offer nor to understand themselves correctly as somehow inter-connected and inter-dependent on each other. As a result these works of human reason lay in tombs covered with the dust of time, tombs that are monuments of their ineffective positions.

A moral framework is so much more than the identification of certain actions to be avoided. It is a view of the human person that should drive a natural way of being, which will ensure the fulfillment of our natures and which should be concerned with the unencumbered expressions of our dignity as the basis for the life of the human community.

I realize that the era of taking seriously the reality of evil, except as entertainment is passed. I believe that this is both dangerous to our ongoing survival and to our capacities to see the truth, embrace it and let it guide our lives. All one has to do is to look and listen to the news, to which many appear to be addicted and at the same time incapable of hearing it. Young men and women sacrifice their lives in order to kill others who are often innocent of any involvement with an enemy which these youth appear so eager to die to defeat.

Our society, once considered to be the last bastion of Christian ideals, no longer embraces the un-compromising belief that human life in any condition is sacred. This position from which it once was believed no one should ever retreat is now accepted as all other human ideas which are capable of being reasoned through, parsed and qualified. It is so very common for people to speak of the "quality" of life as what is really the *summum bonum*. Others seem comfortable weighing suffering against human life. Sometimes it is the suffering of the individual and other times the suffering of those around them that are placed on the scale and weighed against the value of a life.

In any situation in which a human life is set against some other reality to determine its value, one must be very sure that the value against which human life is weighed makes sense. The framework that has been presented has sought to question such realities as suffering, my own and those of others, as making sense as counterweights to human existence. Quality is also both vague and seemingly incongruent as a counter weight to life. Both of these ask the larger question of what really is being placed on that balance. Is it our selfishness, our lack of capacity to be generous, courageous and gifts? In some instances could it be complicated by the lack of communal support so often required in instances where the weight of caring requires others to aid in bearing what an individual is being called to? By asking these questions we are being asked to assess who we are as individuals and as community. When the value of human life is slowly chipped away what can this say about the society of humans who are engaged in this process? It is horrific enough to consider what we are doing to our earth which is our home, but what does it portend when we begin striking out at our very selves?

To assert the supreme value of human life is not to deny the real suffering that may be implied by that assertion. Pain—physical and emotional—is real, both for those suffering it and those around them. Nor is the point to assert a "stiff upper lip" false bravery or to encourage the seeking of pain as a form of false martyrdom. Individuals and societies which proclaim the value of life take upon themselves, by their very proclamation, the obligation to alleviate suffering and to improve the quality of life for individuals and groups. This responsibility has very real social, political and economic implications and is not merely an idea to be embraced intellectually or emotionally.

One does not have to focus only on geopolitical battles that ensnare the young idealists or even the crisis of the sanctity of human life. All one has to do is to look at our cities and the death counts tallied from our own streets. Certainly, most of these tragedies are prompted from different places.

Some are the result of the unfathomable imbalance of means across our country. Entire groups of young men and women, who can see no alternative by which they would be able to participate in the seeming bounty of our culture, choose alternative routes both high in risk and apparently equally high in potential reward. Ironically this articulation sounds like basic economics and the laws of the stock markets. In a sense this is exactly what it is. For it is in the creation of their own sub-economies based on drugs, guns and other weapons of destruction, sex workers, and various other valued products that they create a place for themselves, a potential future outside the rat infested hovels and the alternative of a life of menial labor.

In this parallel world, where what is valued may be different, there is a thriving economy. It is an economy with levels and promotions as well as the capacity to become very affluent. It is in its own way a completely separate social structure with its own rules, values and methods for achieving what for many seems impossible in the larger society. Even the signs of wealth and power are unique and often displayed through expensive custom cars, or garish pieces of jewelry. Sometimes who one is, as expressed by what sub-group one belongs to, is tattooed on one's body as an indicator of both loyalty and commitment now imbedded in one's flesh.

The values of this world are loyalty, respect, production and yes, as always, money. It is strange that, at first sight, these values do not appear twisted. In fact, many of us would be the first to espouse these values as part of the very societies in which we live. The difference is that in the larger society these values are meant to be kept within the proper constraints of the core values that enable us to claim we are civilized. Outside of the more encompassing set of human and social values such as truth, service, love, personal generosity and concern for our neighbor the values of production, economies and labor would be descriptive of monsters, for they would express a view of humanity based on creating external value in lieu of any internal awareness.

As depicted on such serial dramas as The Sopranos, this life of the underworld is very realistically displayed for huge audiences. It is ironic that the quaint sitcoms of the sixties, which often portrayed an over-simplified nuclear family, has now been replaced by shows that do not attempt to hold back on displaying the underbelly of human evil. Through the popularizing of these shows they cease to be shocking. Soon they are part of our family's entertainment.

More frightening than any show which might be produced, is the fact that the moral core of our society and the moral basis for the societies that thrive just under ours, are becoming less distinguishable. What we so euphemistically call "white collar crime" is often indicative of the same moral positions as those held by gangs and organized crime. The desire for money and power has emerged as the twenty-first century's most valued reality. White collar crime is how one can come by it within the social structure of society. If what brings you wealth is not accepted by society, you are merely pushed into one of our many sub-cultures where the same values of money and power can be persued with fewer restrictions. Far be it for us to have to admit that the subcultures and our main culture are merging slowly and that without our conscious choices to do something and be something more, there is little to hold back this trend.

In what now seems like lifetimes ago a fresh young preacher, who was human to his core, but tried to master his inward brokenness if by no other means than consistently speaking to our young men and women about their capacity to make a new and better tomorrow, spoke the following quote,

I am convinced that if we are to get on the right side of the world revolution, we as a nation must undergo a radical revolution of values. We must rapidly begin the shift from a thing-oriented society to a person-oriented society. When machines and computers, profit motives and property rights are considered more important than people, the giant triplets of racism, extreme materialism, and militarism are incapable of being conquered. (Martin Luther King, Jr., http://www.rethinkingschools.org/special_reports/sept11/16_02/sile162.shtml)

Where are our leaders today? Who is inspiring our young, middle aged and elderly to the challenge each is called to face in their own ways? Without the words, resounding in our ears to grasp life's truth with all that one has, this call to be more than I am will never be heard. We need men and women we can believe in who are willing to be more than they are and whose words thus echo in the deepest recesses of our souls.

If no one articulates for me a view of myself that is worth more than what I can take; if I happen to be born to a family that can just barely make ends meet and is without a role model, who can make apparent that I can be any more than what I perceive around me and the circumstances in which I find myself, then what hope is there? For there is the highest probability that I will have a TV and I will be able to see a side of the world that is both compelling and yet so very far from where I am. I may start school and I may even do well, but it will not be long before I become aware of all of the many steps I will need to take just to be at the bottom step of what I desire, and become aware of the many obstacles which may well lie ahead. As a result, many will be tempted to take the easier paths. Without the voices of the angels, who will sing the wonder of this one child? How will we draw him out and away from the siren songs of the devil's promise of an easier way? Who will give these untold innocents hope?

The reason that service was placed at the core of this reflection is that it encompasses an orientation toward life that is both open to it and engendering of it. Through reflecting on service we have forced a reflection on a life orientation. It has been an orientation that is outwardly directed. It has been an orientation of letting go and giving away in opposition to grasping and hoarding what one can get. As its first act, we have learned that service requires an initial gift of one's attention. This attention, while it always has two points of direction, inward and outward, is gift when it is outwardly focused. In many ways, this initial facet of service seems trite, but, as many of us can attest, it is probably the most difficult gift of ourselves. Many of us live in our heads. Most of us focus most of our attending on ourselves, our jobs, concerns, hopes. Few of us would be comfortable with not filling every moment with newspapers, iPods, TV, the internet, just dwelling in reflective silence.

Being attuned to others requires that we create a space in which we can and do discover silence. It is a discipline that necessitates that we turn off, put down and let go of those things that rattle around in our heads. It is a discipline which starts by desiring peace and then the taking of time to make space for it. Initially, it can be very frustrating. One sits quietly and still, allowing the innumerable images, ideas and thoughts to flow past one's consciousness as one would a movie. Few of us would seek to stop the movie to peer at a single frame. In the same way we must let the things that emerge respectfully pass by. Over time this practice of dwelling will slow us down. It will slowly bridge the chasm between the now and where we usually exist. Only as this gap begins to close can one begin to be attuned to self and other in a way that enables one to experience what is. Through this dwelling we slowly emerge closer and closer to the now in which we actually live and where we can meet our God. It is also within this now that we can discover others as they are. It is only in this now that we can embrace life by offering ourselves to others genuinely, without presuppositions and openly. It is within this context that we can begin to see what is needed and how we should respond.

Each of us has been blessed with life. Each of us has a role to play in the unfolding of life. Each of us is an essential player in the redemption of our world and ourselves. Our inter-connectedness as *communio* in its profundity necessitates our re-establishing the truth of our oneness. If it helps, we are like atoms moving about in our orbits, but incapable of being any more than what we are without our coming together in service.

The above explications of the two alternative methods of orienting one's life, each being the polar extreme of any discussion of moral living, may have seemed highly abstract and less than specific enough to provide the clarity and simplicity of hoped-for rules of right living. For many this sense of there not having been enough specificity may well be the result of having been weaned on the juridical lists of "do's" and "don'ts", each having been assigned an appropriate weight that would enable clear classifications. While one might understand the longing for apparent moral clarity associated with act-centered morality, it must also be understood that this apparent exactitude was often at the expense of a real moral appreciation of the human person as actor. It cannot be stressed enough, however, that what we do is always an outcome of who we are and how we see and make sense of our lives. For this reason, focusing on the internal nature of the human person, while it may appear to be a valueless abstraction, is essential to genuine moral understanding. This reality must always be appreciated and believed with its counter-point, which is that we are and must be appreciated as actors. Our internal dispositions are essential in understanding the complete picture of why we act and to appreciate the completeness of our actions or lack thereof.

> The good man brings good things out of the good stored up in him, and the evil man brings evil things out of the evil stored up in him. (Matthew 12:35)

It is for this reason that the ways delineated in this reflection have stepped away from actions as the sole moral indicators of any individual life. This reflection on humanity's moral nature has developed around the fact that human actions should be appreciated as derived from one's internal dispositions, which are comprised of the meanings that both shape how the individual experiences the world and how he experiences himself. Human actions are always the outcome of humanity's free capacity to determine how one is present to reality. Even when these internal realities may not be completely appreciated by us.

The importance of appreciating the nature of the human person as a being whose acts are in no way being denied. What is being held fast to is the fact that all our actions are derived from our internal orientation which includes the ongoing dialogue between our experiences and our capacity to shape these experiences as my own through the meanings I ascribe to them. Thus true appreciation of human nature as an ongoing dialectic between our interiority and the external context in and through which each person comes to their existential awareness is absolutely essential.

It is for this reason that we have stressed the communal facet of our natures as not only unavoidable, but at the heart of our ongoing communication of the truths of who we are and how we come to more complete self understanding and self expression. It is always with this awareness that the seriousness of our messages, both implicit and explicit, to the young are so important, for they often absorb uncritically our individual and societal messages, which may take considerable time for correction. Unfortunately, this is how bigotry, hatred, cynicism, hedonism and the radical individualism which is at the core of so many of our cultural distortions are often conveyed.

At the heart of this reflection on *The Way of Service* is the unquestionable and necessary reality that the human person is the most sacred expression of God's creative generosity. At no time and in no circumstance will the centrality of this truth ever be abrogated. It is an apodictic statement without qualification. No categorization by man, governments or nation states can ever sidestep this central reality.

Unfortunately, it is to a world in which these truths have been forgotten, or worse, are no longer believed, that they must be spoken of and preached as the core of our re-evangelization. The twentieth century was in many respects an abomination. The sacred reality of the human person and the inviolable worth of each human life were not only repeatedly denied, but entire nation states were defined by hatred and the radical and explicit denial of the spiritual aspects of reality.

It is our requirement and our call to bring an end to this past. We must re-establish the universal and undeniable sacredness of each and every person. At the same time we must reignite the passion which must exist at the core of our communities to protect what is sacred no matter its color, sexuality, creed, nationality or any other spurious reason we seem to devise to separate and isolate each other. Nor can we allow the outdated arguments of the rights of sovereign states to engage in systematic genocide while we sit back and ponder potential economic ramifications.

The dignity of the human person was established in our creation when the very spirit of God was breathed into our inanimate shells as the source of our vivication. It was then pronounced unequivocally when we were all declared to be created *ad imago Dei*, or to the image of God. Even Cane, who slew his brother out of human jealousy, was protected by God.

The Lord said, "What have you done? The voice of your brother's blood cries to me from the ground. Now you are cursed because of the ground, which has opened its mouth to receive your brother's blood from your hand. From now on, when you till the ground, it won't yield its strength to you. You shall be a fugitive and a wanderer in the earth." Cain said to the Lord, "My punishment is greater than I can bear. Behold, you have driven me out this day from the surface of the ground. I will be hidden from your face, and I will be a fugitive and a wanderer in the earth. It will happen that whoever finds me will kill me." The Lord said to him, "Therefore whoever slays Cain, vengeance will be taken on him sevenfold." The Lord appointed a sign for Cain, lest any finding him should strike him. Cain went out from the

Lord's presence, and dwelt in the land of Nod, on the east of Eden. (Genesis 4: 10-16)

It is this basic human dignity that is at the core of *The Way of Service*. It is a dignity that acknowledges both human freedom and human responsibility. It is a dignity of far greater worth than a pair of sneakers, membership in a gang or a healthy stock portfolio. The responsibility to live in a constant awareness of each other's sacredness was tied to the very first commandment to love our God with all our hearts and souls. Through the reflections of the Old and New Testaments it became clear that a life in denial of the dignity of the human person could never be a life true to the first and supreme command.

The second aspect of the great command of the New Testament is broken into two inter-related pieces with neither the first nor the second taking on an ordinal preference. The first is the command to a proper love of self. This entails a love of self as a gift of God. It is a love of self that is humble in its truth, patient in its practice and open to the reality of God's ongoing call within the ordinary context of one's life. The second dimension of this command is to love others as one love's oneself. It is the acceptance of the primacy of our sacredness as passed on from our creator and thus the natural appreciation of the sacredness of our God at the center of every human person.

The command to love each other is not the impossible command to like each other, but to do the good that I may see for the other with generosity and humility, regardless of my feelings. It is within this context that the reality of all of God's people, of every race, religion, and social standing as members of the *communio,* or communion of God's children is revealed. It is this *communio* that establishes a social dimension to our moral framework. It envelops humanity in the warm embrace of the charge to each of us to serve our brothers and sisters wherever and however this call can be manifest. In a world where the bounds of communication and awareness find no limit, this call must be exercised through participation in our governments in our societies and local communities.

For some, this call may indeed entail the direct call to go to the farthest ends of the earth to protect human dignity and fight on its behalf. For others, it will be the call to respond to the all too familiar human degradation that is poverty, loneliness, isolation and the lack of basic human needs right in our neighborhoods or cities. Neither is more genuine, neither is higher, for both are authentic responses to the heart of social injustice.

The twenty first century has the means of its own self destruction. Developed through the focus and resources of a world duped into believing that there can ever be an end to the truth "that the man who lives by the sword shall die by the sword" (Mathew 26:52). Now is the time and imperative for humanity to refocus our seemingly unlimited capacities on resolving unacceptable human issues, to come together and make all the resources required available to address the myriad of human indignities that give birth to hatred, revenge, and the ultimate loss of the human soul.

Hunger, human suffering, the incomprehensible injustice of the inequitable distribution of basic human needs, and the inevitable belief that one is disenfranchised and invisible are the source of so many lost lives. The following quotation from

Marianne Williamson, the author of *A Return to Love,* expresses a unique perspective upon the topics upon which we have been reflecting. It is the mirror image of the argument we have been taking. It is equally true and to the degree that it is a source of our inability to raise ourselves to the full height of our beings it must be considered.

Our deepest fear is not that we are inadequate. Our deepest fear is that we are powerful beyond measure. It is our light, not our darkness, that most frightens us. We ask ourselves, Who am I to be brilliant, gorgeous, talented, fabulous? Actually, who are you not to be? You are a child of God. Your playing small doesn't serve the world. There's nothing enlightened about shrinking so that other people won't feel insecure around you. We are all meant to shine, as children do. We were born to make manifest the glory of God that is within us. It's not just in some of us; it's in everyone. And as we let our own light shine, we subconsciously give other people permission to do the same. As we're liberated from our own fear, our presence automatically liberates others.

(Williamson, Marianne, *A Return to Love,* Harper, NY, 1996)

In the same way, our earth, for which we are the custodians, cries out for humanity to face years of stripping its rich abundance away and spewing garbage into the air, the sea and the land upon which we live. Time is no longer our friend. Years of actively disregarding our abuses in order to enable our continued capacities to amass fortunes, has come to an end. The cost of human selfishness has reached the point of repayment. The truth that we are the same everywhere has played itself out again. So much of the culture that defines who we are and for which we are responsible is now reaping what it has sown. Our humanity and our world lay before us as undeniable victims of the loss of our souls.

Before we continue to address the individual calls to respond to the reality of human dignity, it is essential to re-emphasize that there can be no true humanism that is not based on one's firm acceptance of God as our creator and the inherent equality of all humans, which is derived therefrom. Humanism based on human logic and a rationale alone has shown itself to be lacking.

The limits of human judgment have been manifest when humans rely on their own often-self-interested and narrow capacities to draw frightening distinctions that parse the human family into those not truly human for one reason or another. There can be no valid justification for denying the sacred dignity of the human person. History is replete with ongoing manifestations of this error in examples such as discrimination based on nationality, ethnicity, race, sexuality, religion, gender and other spurious methods of denying or restricting the personhood of any individual.

The Way of Service is not merely a framework for social justice, however. It is as essentially a framework for our personal understanding of our call to right living.

We love because he first loved us. If anyone says, "I love God," and hates his brother, he is a liar; for he who does not love his brother whom he has seen cannot love God whom he has not seen. And this commandment we have from him: whoever loves God must also love his brother (1 John 4:19-21)

It is this intricate connection between our God who has loved us and our call to love both Him and our brothers and sisters that is at the very heart of a life of service.

The human person rightly oriented to the two great commands must learn to see themselves and all others as God sees them. This is to appreciate each human being as a tabernacle in which the Spirit of our God resides.

The values of our cultures can often distort our vision such that we see others through a lens oriented toward beauty and thus disdainful of those who may lack this gift. Others can view through the lens of intelligence, or cleverness and be blinded by those who may be in most need of our intellectual talents. Others may view their fellow humans through the lens of selfish preoccupation, or a lens sensitized to those who are appreciated as special in the eyes of the larger society. Many times the lens humans perceive through can completely block the indigent, needy, abandoned or alienated and lonely. Our call is to identify and remove the lenses that occlude us from perceiving the totality of our shared humanity and our call to respond.

Once we are in the position to perceive things as they are and to assess our choices in the light of truth, then we must dig deep within our hearts and souls and discover the inherent love that is the only source of true generosity. It is a falsehood that this generosity must be grand in scale. It is one of the lies set on thwarting the right act that whispers quietly in our ears that there is nothing we can really do. It is a lie that tells us that the problem is far too large for us to even place a dent in it. All that is being asked is that we respond with what we can do. This may be stopping by the side of a homeless person wrapped against the bitter cold and taking them to a local diner and buying them a full meal and a hot cup of coffee. Every good outcome begins with one small act. Every significant transformation begins with a first step.

Our call to respond to human need can often go no farther than our front door, for it can be a refocusing of the energy and love with which one participates in one's family. It can entail the re-energizing of the centrality of our relationship with our partners as well as the commitment to spend additional time with our children, not busy in the study, but fully engaged and a part of their lives. It might mean less time passively ensconced in our favorite chair in front of the TV and the finding of additional ways to do things with our children that might engage their minds and imaginations.

The individual embracing of *The Way of Service* is the result of the exercise of one's free will. As such it requires that one truly have the determination to discover the meaning of being human as articulated in both the Old and New Testaments. It means taking the time to dwell and to assess one's life on a daily basis and to bring to the fore both one's successes and one's failures. It requires that one spend time in meditation so that one can slow down and slowly learn to live in the moment. It entails slowly gaining control of one's mind as a way of focusing on the moment and thus being able to bring the full recourses of who one is and who one may be called to be to the fore. In this way it begins with the self. As Jesus made clear,

> For this reason I say to you, do not be worried about your life, as to what you will eat or what you will drink; nor for your body, as to what you will put on. Is not life more than food, and the body more than clothing?

"Look at the birds of the air, that they do not sow, nor reap nor gather into barns, and yet your heavenly Father feeds them. Are you not worth much more than they? And who of you by being worried can add a single hour to his life? (Matthew 6:25)

Only through learning to trust in God and to let go of the senseless worrying which only takes years from one's life and never addresses the source of one's concern can we garner the internal strength we need to live authentically and to be ready to respond with what our life presents us. It is always and everywhere a matter of the choice of each person. This choice is always one's own and cannot be taken from you. Yes, it can be a choice to disengage and it can entail the slow blocking of our senses through a variety of addictions. The one choice modern humanity has demonstrated as easy to make is the shutting out of our world, ourselves and even those we claim to love.

Discovering the values one seeks to live, which are often in direct contradiction to one's culture, entails exposing oneself to these counter-cultural values, through reading and meditation. If, therefore, one is seeking to make real these values in one's life, it is essential to become increasingly familiar with our God. This is not done by racing through Gospel readings. It is only achieved through reading in such a way as to enable the depth of what is being communicated to sink ever deeper into one's heart, where it must take up its place and where it must make its home.

It is also seldom helpful to quote the New Testament as a way of getting others to see its value and follow it. One's actions are the only real expression of service. Too many false preachers have watered down the power and radical nature of the life of Jesus. In the larger context of the loss of the value of our words, the word of God made man has not escaped this radical deflation in meaning. Only through being the type of person Jesus calls all of us to be, will Christ be noticed. When people ask why you are the way you are, you will we be able to speak from the authority of an inner truth.

Ever weary of the temptation to seem rather than to be, we must strive unflinchingly to internalize who we are and who we want to be. Always being aware of the trap of the ego centered follower who seeks to be noticed, seen and thus to gain a place of respect and prominence, we must embrace the interiority of truth in opposition to its exterior appearances.

When he noticed how the guests picked the places of honor at the table, he told them this parable: "When someone invites you to a wedding feast, do not take the place of honor, for a person more distinguished than you may have been invited. If so, the host who invited both of you will come and say to you, 'Give this man your seat.' Then, humiliated, you will have to take the least important place. But when you are invited, take the lowest place, so that when your host comes, he will say to you, 'Friend, move up to a better place.' Then you will be honored in the presence of all your fellow guests. For everyone who exalts himself will be humbled, and he who humbles himself will be exalted. (Luke 14: 7-11)

Lest one walk away from this reflection discouraged and filled with the overpowering sense of one's smallness in the face of such seemingly large issues; it is critical to grasp the simplicity of *The Way of Service*. For what it necessitates is only our own conversion. The transformation of our world begins with the transformation of one person, a transformation enabled within the context of communal service and love.

It requires the capacity to say "no" to what is merely popular. It requires the ability to look hard and long at ourselves. To ask the very hard questions of who we are and who we are being asked to be. It necessitates the honesty of seeing the truth and then the simple act of choosing to be authentic in the next moment and after that the next and onwards.

Never become overly attached to your past. Never let your mistakes and your wasted years keep you from having the courage to be more in the next moment. Our God writes straight with crooked lines. Our narratives are never complete until we die. The question of what narrative is being written by us and whether it is the story we wish to leave has no better time for being determined than today.

O Lord, you have searched me and known me!
You know when I sit down and when I rise up;
you discern my thoughts from afar.
You search out my path and my lying down
and are acquainted with all my ways.
Even before a word is on my tongue,
behold, O Lord, you know it altogether.
You hem me in, behind and before,
and lay your hand upon me.
Such knowledge is too wonderful for me;
it is high; I cannot attain it.
Where shall I go from your Spirit?
Or where shall I flee from your presence?

If I ascend to heaven, you are there!
If I make my bed in Sheol, you are there!
If I take the wings of the morning
and dwell in the uttermost parts of the sea,
even there your hand shall lead me,
and your right hand shall hold me.
If I say, "Surely the darkness shall cover me,
and the light about me be night."
even the darkness is not dark to you;
the night is bright as the day,
for darkness is as light with you.
For you formed my inward parts;
you knitted me together in my mother's womb.
I praise you, for I am fearfully and wonderfully made.
Wonderful are your works;
my soul knows it very well.
My frame was not hidden from you,
when I was being made in secret,
intricately woven in the depths of the earth.
Your eyes saw my unformed substance;
in your book were written, every one of them,
the days that were formed for me,
when as yet there was none of them.
How precious to me are your thoughts, O God!
How vast is the sum of them!
If I would count them, they are more than the sand.
I awake, and I am still with you.
Oh that you would slay the wicked, O God!
O men of blood, depart from me!
They speak against you with malicious intent;
your enemies take your name in vain!
Do I not hate those who hate you, O Lord?
And do I not loathe those who rise up against you?
I hate them with complete hatred;
I count them my enemies.

Search me, O God, and know my heart!
Try me and know my thoughts!
And see if there be any grievous way in me,
and lead me in the way everlasting!
(Psalm 139)

CONCLUSION

The preceding chapters have all focused on delivering a moral framework that could stand solidly on the foundation of the human person that was set forth in *The Will to Love* and carried forward. It is a view of the human person as an end in itself. It accepts at humanity's core, our freedom, which is both the source of our perceptions and our actions, for it is a freedom that is inherently constitutive. As a result it is a view of humanity that necessitates our accepting our radical responsibility and culpability.

This view of humanity required an understanding of the right use of our gifts. In this reflection the purpose was to make explicit what the right uses of our gifts are. Our answer has been clear: we are called to a life of mutual service and love. This has required that we accept the truth of our natures as being communal and thus highly interconnected. It has articulated our challenge, which is to examine ourselves honestly and determine what is that from which we operate and see reality. Is it our selfish needs and concerns or have we had the strength to discover our capacity to see as our God sees and to love as He has loved us.

This moral framework has required us to look at where our hearts lie and thus to be clear as to that which drives our meanings and actions. We have been challenged to accept the sorry state of our culture. We have been asked to reassess our

212

part in what is and to ascertain if we are truly being all that we must be in these times to ensure that what is true can once again determine our values and color our dreams. It is a moral framework that has not asked us to make any drastic choices unless we have come to be aware that we are being asked to do so. It has, however, asked us to be open to the very real acts of generosity and self offering that may be asked of us.

This reflection has been painfully clear that Christians have abandoned the Christ that so many of us have said is a significant part of our lives and who we are. This reflection has made explicit the fact that the majority of those of us who would call ourselves Christian have abandoned Him who offered up all for our lives. As a moral framework it has not gotten sidetracked by the often absurd legalistic approaches to human life that have rendered religion as apparently irrelevant to so many lives. We have instead gone back to the way of Christ, which looked more at what drove one to act in a certain way, i.e. the interiority of truth in opposition to the exterior appearance of acts.

This framework for a Christian morality has not foolishly taken the easy shots at religion, but reiterated that as always, it is a human institution seeking to give expression to the spiritual realities so essential to human life. It should not be abandoned for its incompleteness, but should be embraced for what is from above and forgiven for what is from that part of us always in need of our honest assessments and control. For the symbolic expressions of our real internal faith must have methods for its genuine expression, not just for each of us individually, but most essentially for the communal essence that we are and that is our only hope.

213

This moral framework has asked us to look with our eyes and heart at where we are and to where we are headed. It has offered to each of us the opportunity to take the initial steps of humility which will enable us to alter the paths we have trodden in the hope that we can recapture our inherent dignity as sacred individuals and as sacred members of the human family. By so doing it will require relooking at our values and having the courage to let go of those which may have seemed correct, but which, under closer scrutiny, have displayed their inherent flaws.

This moral framework has set as central to our capacity to alter our courses the fighting for and focus on the re-capturing of our families. It has merely touched the potential cost of letting this deterioration continue. It requires that we look straight on at those messages with which our young minds are being filled with through that which is presented as entertainment and in the omnipresent marketing machine. We must be responsible for the gift of universal communication and not just be passive to its presence. Through asking ourselves what it is that is forming our ideas and our values it is essential that we discern that which is forming who and what kind of people we are.

As a moral framework this reflection has also presented us with methods of being re-introduced to what we believe should be shaping our capacities to understand life through the meanings we give it. It has expressly identified the distortions of control, manipulation and the warped views of the human process of living that are central to the lie of modern western culture. Such essential aspects of human life as suffering and death have been removed from their places within a well grounded and mature acceptance of the human condition and as a result rage has grown in us as the twisted result of our expectation that we should not have to face these human conditions. It has also twisted our sense of what is essential and what we should be teaching our children by embracing a belief in control that is an illusion.

Only by slowing down and allowing ourselves to re-engage with reality from a new perspective can we possibly let go and come to understand the real alternatives to the way we have set up our communities, our larger societies as well as our nation states. The mystery of the conundrum of humanity as both an end in itself and yet dependent on the community for its proper emergence is essential for us to grasp. The radical individualism that has been expressed as the "me generation" is a lie that poisons our souls and inhibits our capacity to emerge from the call we have accepted.

What is most essential to all of this is the reality that hope is not lost. As the object of faith, hope remains active and as real as ever, but it is the outcome of faith. It is the outcome of faith in ourselves and in each other. It is an outcome of our faith in God, which may take time for some of us to re-appropriate after years of experiencing the misuse of His name. It is a faith that can enable a posture of forgiveness; a forgiveness that is essential in being offered to ourselves and then to one another. It is the realization which, through the process of forgiving will expose the absolute irrationality of judgment of ourselves and anyone else. It will illuminate the full dignity and sacredness of every human being as that wonderful place where God chooses to tabernacle with us.

All through this process we will be asked over and over to not be afraid, in the same way that Jesus told his followers not to fear. It is fear that build walls. It is fear that separates and ostracizes. Only through trust as the replacement of fear will we enable the outstretched arms of the crucified Christ to truly embrace all. As a result, we will no longer need to live with absurd ideas such as "love the sinner hate the sin". We must love each other as the unity we are and as the incomplete process of unfolding that we are. Sin is and always will be a part of our world. Removing sin will only be achieved by love.

While this moral framework has not proclaimed with singular focus the sins possible to humanity, it has instead articulated an alternative orientation to life and to living that leaves sin to its proper place as part of the process of coming into a fuller appreciation of who we are and how we are meant to express our inherent dignity in this world. We are not naïve; the reality of sin is all too familiar to most of us, but our focus cannot and should not be on it, but on love which conquers all sin.

The kind of transformation that is required for each of us and our world is of such a very different scope and orientation that only our re-embracing of a mature and real understanding of love as a willed choice and commitment can begin to address the transformation which is required. All the various aspects of love that have been identified such as service, being attuned, generosity, self offering, living in the present, letting go, creating real communities, and being available and selfless are but a few of the initial skirmishes that must take place in our taking back of our dignity. In the process we have the possibility of healing ourselves, the broken communities and world in which we live.

Life is inherently purposeful. It requires a balanced soberness in the way we embrace each moment with which we are blessed. As a gift, we are asked to appreciate and respect not only our lives, but the lives of all who are equally gifts. As with any gift we should cherish it in its free offering to us. The best manner in which we can give thanks to the giver is by being in turn gifts to each other. Within this reality of our giftedness there is no such thing as entitlement. We are gifts given in order that we might be offered as gifts ourselves.

A PRAYER

People are often unreasonable,
Illogical, and self-centered;
Forgive them anyway.
If you are kind,
People may accuse you of selfish, ulterior motives;
Be kind anyway.
If you are successful,
You will win some false friends and some true enemies;
Succeed anyway.
If you are honest and frank,
People may cheat you;
Be honest and frank anyway.
What you spend years building,
Someone could destroy overnight;
Build anyway.
If you find serenity and happiness,
Others may be jealous;
Be happy anyway.
The good you do today,
People will often forget tomorrow;
Do good anyway.
Give the world the best you have,
And it may never be enough;
Give the world the best you've got anyway.
You see, in the final analysis,
It is between you and God;
It was never between you and them anyway.
(Attributed to Mother Teresa)
Amen

Breinigsville, PA USA
15 February 2011
255635BV00001B/26/P